KU-845-249

Charles E. Jacob
Vassar College

LEADERSHIP
IN THE
NEW
DEAL

The
Administrative
Challenge

Prentice-Hall, Inc., Englewood Cliffs, New Jersey

All rights reserved. No part of this book may be reproduced in any form or by any means without permission in writing from the publisher.

Current printing (last digit):
10 9 8 7 6 5 4 3 2 1

C

© 1967 by PRENTICE-HALL, INC.
Englewood Cliffs, New Jersey

Library of Congress Catalog Card No.: 67-12249

Printed in the United States of America

EDITOR'S FOREWORD

Leadership in the New Deal: The Administrative Challenge is a volume in the American Historical Sources Series: Research and Interpretation, a series devoted to the exploration of aspects of American history and to the process of interpreting historical evidence. The introduction to each volume will be followed by some of the key documents used to prepare the essay. Readers are thus invited to share in the experience of turning raw evidence into history. The essays have been written especially for this series and represent contributions to historical knowledge as well as demonstrations in the writing of history based upon sources included in the work.

In 1933, when Franklin Roosevelt became President, the Depression was so severe as to appear to many a businessman, worker, and economist to be on the verge of a general economic collapse. Such a collapse would have laid bare to attack all American institutions and traditions. Faced with this prospect, the new President knew that he must act. The programs initiated and the agencies created to run them are well known. But were these programs in any sense part of a coherent long-range plan, were they effective, could the executive branch of the government effectively control and direct so many agencies? Historians have debated these points.

Professor Jacob does not claim to have found the answers to these questions, but in the essay and the sources that follow we find evidence to suggest that pragmatism did not mean lack of program, that the President enlisted not only many administrators but also good

▼

ones, and that in his own novel way Roosevelt effectively made use of the quantity and quality of talent attracted to Washington in the 1930's. In this book we get some fascinating views of the people who made the New Deal. Success or failure of the New Deal to meet the challenge of the Depression becomes a matter of carrying out policy as well as formulating it.

Big government has become a fact of American life. The complicated ways in which that government works must be carefully examined if we are to understand the decision-making process at the national level of government.

In this essay Professor Jacob offers us a view of the complicated process of establishing, organizing, and controlling an administrative apparatus. As we seek to understand American history in the recent past we will find this type of administrative history invaluable.

LORMAN RATNER

Hunter College

CONTENTS

vii

LEADERSHIP
IN THE
NEW
DEAL

Administrative Leadership: Challenge and Response

The mood of the American people in 1932 was a mixture of desperation and uncertainty fostered by the apparent inability of leadership—both in private life and in government—to deal with the malaise of economic depression. In this atmosphere the people grasped the hope offered by Franklin D. Roosevelt and elected to the presidency the one man who seemed ready and determined to provide leadership adequate to the demands of the crisis. The years that followed that momentous act of political choice were to reward amply the popular quest for leadership. Political foe and friend alike could agree that one thing the Roosevelt New Deal did offer was leadership. To some this meant enlightenment and progress; to others it constituted a dread trek down the road to collectivism and dictatorship.

Although some of the ends and many of the by-products of the Roosevelt revolution may be weighed in the balance of one's political and social values and found wanting, a less controversial and perhaps more rewarding inquiry may be directed to the nature of Roosevelt's political leadership in fashioning the historic results. Yet the subject of political leadership—even the political leadership of one President—is so broad that it requires a systematic investigation of different *aspects* of political leadership.

A President must have skill in communicating his goals to the people, arousing their interest, and inducing their support. In other words, he must shape public opinion. Because policy-making power in the United States is divided among different branches of government, the President must also be both a legislative strategist and tactician in order to shape congressional behavior toward his policy goals. Furthermore, a President must be more than a nominal leader of his political party to make good use of the partisan energies available for electoral support throughout the nation and the partisan cohesion of his followers in Congress.

Each of these aspects of leadership should be studied closely in evaluating the total political leadership of Roosevelt. But this essay is particularly concerned with still another aspect of that leadership. This aspect may be most properly called administrative leadership and addresses itself to the problems of organization and management within the executive branch itself. Stated simply, one might suggest that Roosevelt had to ask himself two general questions in 1933: What are the outstanding challenges and how should they be confronted? Although Roosevelt had some of his own ideas about the sources and solutions of many of the problems facing his administration, before he could become chief executive of the nation in fact as well as name he had to assemble a body of officials who could help him identify and sort out the complex issues and apply the principles appropriate to dealing with them.

Although recruitment is vital to the political leader, an administration does not automatically function in blissful harmony and cooperation as soon as the appointments have been made. Thus this essay also discusses organizational and personal problems and conflicts that are bound to arise in any bureaucratic context and that were evident from the early days of the New Deal. How Franklin D. Roosevelt dealt with these problems and tensions is the final major theme of this essay.

A brief note should be made about the period. All of the examples given and all of the relations discussed are taken from the early years of the Roosevelt era. This was done in order to confine the essay to manageable bounds. Consequently, no attention is given to possible variations in Roosevelt's style of leadership when, in his own words, he exchanged the title and the mission "Dr. New Deal" for "Dr. Win-the-War." It is felt, however, that more is to be gained by concentrating on the new problems of a new administration as they are confronted in new ways than by attempting to "cover" a presidential epoch.

VARIETIES OF ADMINISTRATORS

Any chief executive creating an administration must, sooner or later, think in terms of the different kinds of jobs to be done and the ideal kinds of people to do them. Different talents and skills are required to conduct the affairs of the nation. The final combination of talents and skills and their use by the President are the essence of his personal leadership. Although the character of an administration reflects the personal orientation of its President, circumstances also determine the choices made by the chief. This principle was well illustrated in 1932.

In that third year of the depression, national income had fallen to less than half its 1929 level. One-quarter of the work force was unemployed. For those who still had jobs, wages had fallen off so sharply that they were in debt almost as severely as the unemployed. Every economic indicator (investment, production, credit, debt, employment, and the rest) told the same pitiful story. From the bread lines to the soup kitchens, from the city reliefers to the dust bowl farmers, came anguished cries for help. The universal negative answer given to the popular lyrical question of the thirties—"Brother, Can You Spare a Dime?"—summed up the situation.

It was a situation that called for imaginative thinking and purposeful action. In his First Inaugural on March 4, 1933, President Roosevelt promised "action, and action now." And it was the necessity for this action that demanded the talents and skills of men with inventive minds and trained in the technical expertise of the social sciences as well as the law. Mere managers or caretakers would no longer satisfy the demands made upon the American government. Roosevelt's creation of the "brains trust" recognized this fact.

This first act of administrative leadership by Roosevelt was actually performed before the election. In 1932, as Governor of New York State, the future President called upon the first of the many public administrators who would advise him in the years to come. In March, 1932, in a conference with his counsel, Sam Rosenman, Roosevelt agreed to the other's suggestion that the time had come to search out expert advice on the nature of the nation's economic problems. Rosenman recommended that FDR consult with Raymond Moley, then a Professor at Columbia

University and an economist known for his progressive leanings. Moley was asked to assemble a group of advisors capable of covering the various areas of economic distress. In turn, Rexford G. Tugwell and Adolf A. Berle, Jr., both Columbia colleagues of Moley, were called in and formed the original brains trust. A close observer of the New Deal from its early origins has written that, although others would come and go, the Moley-Tugwell-Berle team constituted the essential corps of original planners of the New Deal. Actually, the brains trust came to be a much larger group.

The roles played by these advisors depended on the particular problem areas. The general approach to future economic policy was largely set by Moley, Tugwell, and Berle. These scholars shared an important point of view in rejecting the Wilson and Brandeis program for atomizing American business. Rather, the New Deal thinkers accepted big business as natural and even desirable, but in need of regulation. They interpreted the depression as a domestic phenomenon that could be cured by domestic controls. Hence their recipe called for generous extensions of government's regulatory powers (such as stock market regulation and the abolition of child labor) and the development of controls designed to stimulate and stabilize the economy.

After the inauguration, and particularly during the first hundred days, the press corps noticed several other reappearing faces belonging to specialists who served on a widened brains trust. Once the general pattern of moderate planning had been established by Professor Moley and his colleagues, others were called upon to suggest specific policy strategies designed to cope with agricultural, industrial, and monetary problems. Professor M. L. Wilson of Montana State College, who had championed the plan for domestic allotments in agriculture, succeeded in convincing Rex Tugwell of the soundness of this plan to restrict farm production by limiting acreage. In the new administration, Wilson was retained as chief of the Wheat Division of the Department of Agriculture. The group of experts who shaped farm policy in the early New Deal period were, besides Wilson, William I. Myers, a former Professor of Farm Finance at Cornell University; Louis Bean of the staff of the Bureau of Agricultural Economics; and Mordecai Ezekiel, described by a journalist of the times as a "brilliant young economist . . . who can demonstrate by logarithms how to raise hogs."

The crisis in industry and finance called for high-level brainstorming in the early years of the New Deal. In both broad areas of policy, programs were hammered out despite the widely differing views presented by financial, academic, industrial, and legal experts. For a time Professor George F. Warren, a Professor of Farm Management at Cornell, played a very influential role in American monetary policy. Warren's theory argued that the essential cause of the depression was the government's failure to purchase gold which would have raised its price and the general price level. Gold buying would create a "commodity dollar" which would have constant buying power for all commodities. Stability was thus to be brought to the entire economy. Although FDR was convinced of the plausibility of the Warren thesis and even proceeded for several weeks to set the price of gold on a day-to-day basis, the rather innocent and notably unsuccessful experiment was a subject of strong counter-arguments made by such other financial brains trusters as Dean G. Acheson (Under Secretary of the Treasury), James P. Warburg (a Treasury Department financial adviser; and O. W. Sprague, one of the President's old Harvard professors.

Administration planning for industrial recovery brought to the fore still other high-level thinkers. What was to become the National Industrial Recovery Act grew out of the debates and compromises carried on primarily among Hugh Johnson, Donald Richberg, and other top level officials of the administration as well as Moley and Tugwell. Johnson, a former cavalry general and organizer of the draft in World War I and Donald Richberg, a labor attorney and an old-line New Nationalist and Bull Mooser, agreed that laissez faire and the sanctity given to competition needed to be replaced by cooperation under governmental aegis. The NRA which resulted (and which was to be found unconstitutional two years later in 1935) established the private-public "partnership" which FDR had mentioned in the campaign and provided for massive public works projects.

Although business and industry were seen in partnership with the government according to early New Deal intellectual orthodoxy, the financial community merited no such relationship. Most of the bright young men who dealt with the contribution of financial irresponsibility to the depression favored strict public regulation as the proper course of action. Thus when the brilliant Professor of Legislation at the Harvard

Law School, James Landis, and the equally brilliant young Harvard Law graduates, Thomas Corcoran and Benjamin V. Cohen together produced first the Securities Act of 1933 and then the more comprehensive Securities Exchange Act of 1934, a disciplinary approach, as Schlesinger has noted, replaced a propitiating stance. Reporting and disclosure requirements were made in order to regulate trading practices and to combat the problem of manipulations by insiders—a practice disclosed in the Pecora Hearings into the stock market and banking community. The capstone of the structure, the Securities and Exchange Commission, was established to carry out the regulatory function.

The men of vision were of course indispensable to the Roosevelt revolution. But these idea men and political architects were a small group in the whole administrative complex. Their numbers were manifoldly exceeded by those who possessed skills of another sort. This second skill-group was made up of those either trained in, or naturally adept at the task of management and organization on a small scale. These supervisory types, or "bosses," were responsible for getting the grand programs—thought up by the brains trusters and enacted by congress—implemented into reality. And although, as a general class of administrators, their intellects may have been less sparkling than those of the Tugwells, Corcorans, and Berles, the mission they were called upon to perform was equally important and therefore, their peculiar qualities just as valuable. Of course, in a literal sense, the head of each executive department, bureau, agency, administration, commission, authority, or office falls into the category presently under consideration. While the role of each person bearing such an executive title in the New Deal cannot be examined, a few examples may elucidate the contribution of this particular administrative class.

The very nature of the bold, new programs enacted in the flush of New Deal victory in 1933 required imaginative but cautious administrators. The untested provisions of unprecedented policies would require audacity and courage in the administrator; they would also call for extreme integrity and sharp-eyed supervision by those responsible for implementation. The new public works legislation was an instance of policy that particularly demanded these qualities, and they could hardly have been found in better quantity than in the Secretary of Interior, Harold L. Ickes. Ickes, who came to the New Deal at its beginning and remained until after the death of the President twelve years later, was placed in charge of public works at the outset because of his integrity and responsibility. Title II of the National Industrial Recovery Act provided for a Public Works Administration capable of initiating construction projects directly and making loans and grants to the states and other public bodies to encourage construction. At the cabinet level, the President asked Secretary Ickes to be Administrator, a choice which would bear mixed fruits.

"Honest Harold," as he came to be called, firmly held the strings to the $3.3 billion purse initially allocated for public works. Here was a man who trusted no one automatically and who, Schlesinger notes, as PWA Administrator, "read every line of everything and often fired documents back with demands for revision and correction. . . . Ickes meanwhile called on PWA employees to report on each other, denounced them for coming late to work or taking too long for coffee, and even issued an edict against pulling down shades over the windows in office doors."

Even his own peers did not escape the suspicious challenges of the Administrator. When Jesse Jones, Chairman of the Reconstruction Finance Corporation, proposed that the RFC buy certain PWA securities and either guarantee a profit or assume the loss for the PWA, Ickes demanded: "Where's the catch?" Only after convincing his colleague there was no hidden liability was the Chairman of the RFC permitted to handle securities for the PWA—a transaction that turned out to be highly profitable for PWA.

As a consequence of such attitudes and such a general demeanor, Ickes (who even referred to himself as an "old curmudgeon") was less than universally loved. On the other hand, it was difficult not to respect him as a public servant. Though there were those who would argue that, in spite of the schools, roads, dams, hospitals, bridges, and irrigation projects built by PWA, the administration foundered in its economic function of producing jobs at a fast rate, Ickes could ignore them and bask in the reward of his chief's tribute to him. For FDR said in a cabinet meeting in 1934:

> When Harold took hold of public works, he had to start cold. He had no program and he had no organization. It was necessary to develop both. A lot of people thought that all he would have

to do would be to shovel money out of the window. There have been a good many complaints about the slowness of the public works program and Harold's caution. There hasn't been even a minor scandal in public works and that is some record.

There were also instances when Roosevelt based his selection of administrators more on the previous experience and associations of the appointee than on any guarantee of managerial expertise. The naming of Joseph P. Kennedy as first Chairman of the Securities and Exchange Commission was done primarily because of Kennedy's contacts among the elite of the nation's financial community. Indeed, there was much criticism of the appointment on the grounds that Kennedy himself had been guilty of certain practices now proscribed under the new securities legislation and that the famous titan, even though a loyal Democrat, could hardly be trusted to regulate his own kind without fear or favor. But Kennedy fulfilled the hopes of the President and of Raymond Moley, who had recommended his appointment, by vigorous and single-minded reform action. The Commissioner begged, persuaded, badgered, wheedled, and cajoled his former colleagues and competitors in the financial community into accepting SEC regulation and extending cooperation. In the end, not only did the financial community accept SEC regulation, it came to appreciate and take comfort in the order and rationality afforded by the new legislation. That a respected (and feared) member of the Street was in charge from the outset was a great aid in gaining compliance. Decades later, Judge James Landis—originally miffed at the Kennedy appointment and himself later to be Chairman of the Commission—supported this evaluation in an interview reported by Richard Whalen in *The Founding Father*:

> I'd been pounded for a year by the financial interests and I knew how difficult it was going to be to get the SEC off the ground. Kennedy was impressive. *They* would take things from him that they wouldn't take from us reformers. For instance, he could call up the president of Bethlehem Steel or Standard Oil and tell him to send his comptroller around for a little chat, and the fellow would come. At this stage, we didn't have that kind of power. We didn't know who was who.

A vital prerequisite for the establishment of any policy is the co-operation of the legislative branch. Consequently, it is important that certain presidential administrators be on good terms with Congress. Roosevelt understood this and sought to derive maximum benefit from certain of his appointees by virtue of their excellent relations with Congress. Indeed, the retention in office of certain officials by the President may have been determined more by their congressional reputation than the quality of their administrative skills.

An excellent example of this administrative convenience was Cordell Hull, Secretary of State from 1933 to 1944, who could make many claims to that high office, not the least of which was his skill in dealing with Congress. When the President appointed Hull, the sixty-two-year-old Tennessean assumed his duties after twenty-four years' experience on Capitol Hill, all but the previous two of which had been in the House of Representatives. Hull was an old-line Wilsonian, free-trade Democrat, and at one time he had even served as National Chairman of his Party. Although Hull could not always count on the President to support his principles of economic internationalism, the President was always careful not to alienate his Secretary of State. Samuel Rosenman has said that Hull was the one man in public life whose threatened resignation gave the President great concern. In his *Memoirs* Hull describes the process of the proper care and feeding of congressmen, noting that whenever congressmen presented difficulties in their relations with the State Department, the Secretary demanded to be informed and proceeded to deal personally with the problem. Moreover, Hull states in his memoirs:

> I did go occasionally to the Senate and House and drop in on Members to say hello and pay my respects and possibly to have luncheon with them. This was in addition to my regular appearances before the Senate and House committees. These visits were prompted both by my feeling of comradeship for my old associates and by a desire to achieve cooperation and teamwork between Congress and the State Department.

An outstanding example of a presidential "showpiece," or hostage, to conservatives in and out of Congress was Jesse H. Jones, Chairman of the Reconstruction Finance Corporation and later Secretary of Commerce. Jones, a Texas banker and industrialist—and a hold-over from the Hoover Administration—provided what FDR himself described as needed ballast for his administration. Frightening as was the prospect and practice of New Dealers handling millions and billions of dollars and making sweeping economic policies affecting all commerce and industry, the conservative took some solace in the fact that one of the chief economic czars in the Administration was a responsible, free enterprise capitalist of the first order. A long profile of Jones, in *Fortune Magazine* in 1940, concludes that he was really the only reliable businessman working for the administration, the only man capable of understanding and sympathizing with the subtle nuances of the business decision.

As a result of the high regard in which he was held in the business community, Jones exercised an almost hypnotic spell over conservatives in Congress. When he appeared before congressional committees, the dialogue sounded like a mutual admiration society. Senator Arthur Vandenberg of Michigan felt that Jones held the confidence of members of Congress more than any other administration figure. Jones was, of course, aware of his position and the leverage it gave him with the President. He notes in his memoirs that if the President asked him to do something which "we could not or should not do—and that only happened a few times—we just did not do it." His biographer suggests that Jones avoided carrying out Presidential orders with which he disagreed by a resort to "inconspicuous inaction." And the President knew it. The point was that the rewards in the form of congressional accommodation to general administration policy justified even a bit of occasional insubordination in the eyes of the President.

A systematic analysis of different talents and skills in the Roosevelt New Deal would, if left at that, be tidy but historically misleading. At least two warnings should be made. The first concerns the exclusiveness of the categories explored. Of course there was an overlap of skills, talents, and functions. Some of the grand planners and "idea men" were also organizers and managers and even, occasionally, political public relations men. Indeed, if the experience of Raymond Moley is not atypical, even those at the summit of influence and decision-making had to perform almost menial tasks. In his reminiscences Ray Moley discloses that aside from the intellectual tasks of advising the President, writing parts of his speeches articulating administration policies, and engaging in conferences with other brains trusters, he held down his official governmental job as Assistant Secretary in the State Department and helped to relieve the President of the awesome and tedious job of receiving callers who advocated endless variations on reform and policy proposals. In this latter capacity—which Moley considered his least important and most enervating—the intellectual acted as an outer office filter for the President.

A second qualification that must be made concerning categories of administrators is that the man who was ultimately responsible for their selection, the President, surely did not work from a series of charts outlining the functions and skill needs for his official family. But how *were* the bureaucrats picked by the Chief Executive? Or, to rephrase the query, assuming the goal was the "best man for the job," what limitations prevented Roosevelt from reaching it?

The first limitation is the President's need to rely on the judgment of others. Thus, many an administrator was pressed into New Deal service by secondary level selection or cooptation. Hence, as we have seen, the growth of the brains trust began with Moley who then recruited Tugwell and Berle, who in turn called upon their own colleagues and contacts in the academic world. Or, an outsider, such as Bernard Baruch or Felix Frankfurter, would serve sporadically and informally as a personnel agent for the Administration. The outstanding example is Professor Frankfurter—Dean of the Harvard Law School in 1933—who was responsible for the placement of Nathan R. Margold as Solicitor in the Interior Department, Charles Wyzanski, Jr., in the Labor Department, Jerome Frank in the Agricultural Adjustment Administration, Dean G. Acheson in the Treasury Department—to mention but a few of those who would pursue long careers of distinguished public service which they began armed with letters of recommendation from Felix Frankfurter.

Occasionally, the ideal appointments were not made because the favored candidate simply did not want to serve. Moley argues that in 1933 the Republican Party had a near monopoly on experienced and skilled administrators, thus limiting the President's field of choice. FDR himself was unable, for example, to persuade Bernard Baruch to head the

Agricultural Adjustment Agency and had to accept Baruch's recommendation of George Peek for the position, and then only after Peek had extracted the concession that he report directly to the President, thus circumventing his nominal superior, Henry Wallace, Secretary of Agriculture.

Finally, it must be noted that the President's discretion in the shaping of his administration was limited by certain necessary political and "recognition" appointments. Of the former, more has been made of the insidiousness of political appointments than is justified. To be sure, rewards were granted for electoral support but these were relatively insignificant to the whole administration. Furthermore, many New Deal administrators whose appointments were at least partly motivated by political considerations, such as Farley or Kennedy, nevertheless served as effective supporters of overall New Deal policy.

A slightly different manner of appointment is that made for the primary purpose of recognizing a particular region, class, occupation, or other social, economic, or ideological segment of the nation. As we have seen, this principle was involved in the appointment and retention of Jesse Jones. Other representatives of the business and financial elite of the country who held prominent positions in the New Deal government were Lewis Douglas, Director of the Bureau of the Budget and symbol of fiscal integrity; Marriner Eccles, former banker and Roosevelt appointee to the Federal Reserve Board; and, again, Joseph P. Kennedy. Organized social reform (along with womanhood) was recognized in the appointment of Frances Perkins as Secretary of Labor and no less an influence than Harry Hopkins came to the New Deal from a background of social work. One could go on to cite a splendid variety of other groups whose interests were recognized by presidential appointment, such as agriculture, labor, conservation, and so on. The point which needs to be underlined, however, is that even though all major organized interests were taken into account, within these broad imperatives, the President exercised rather a wide range of choice and was able to attract, on the whole, a very high order of dedicated and skillful administrators. Finally FDR even managed to permit himself the luxury of an impulse or snapjudgment in making appointments. To Raymond Moley, Roosevelt's decision in favor of Harold Ickes as Interior Secretary, accompanied by the remark: "I liked the cut of his jib," was akin to an act of whimsey.

INTERNAL ADMINISTRATIVE CONFLICT

The effective pursuit of any political program, and particularly one as ambitious and reformatory as the New Deal, requires a maximum amount of unified, coordinated, consistent work by administrative servants of the program. Yet the very unity and coordination needed were limited by the competing groups flourishing in pluralistic America and represented by the diverse kinds of government aides who set up shop in Washington from 1933 on. Thus the New Dealers were a very motley collection, intellectually, temperamentally, and politically. And the task of leadership was made difficult by a variety of internal conflicts in the Administration. In order to set the stage for an examination of Roosevelt's brand of leadership, some of the sources of administrative conflict must be scanned.

Four important problems of the many that can arise in administration were: ideological differences; differences in strategy and methodology; differences and conflicts in personality and status; and the basic organizational or institutional problems endemic to all large organizations.

One clear focus of ideological conflict in the early years of the New Deal was agricultural policy. As in all other areas of the economy, it was almost universally accepted that *something* had to be done. The nation's farmers were among the most grievous sufferers of the depression. Industrial depression brought a decline in the demand for agricultural commodities at home, and there was also a decline in foreign buying that further reduced the farmer's market. The critical fall of prices made it more and more difficult for the farmers to pay their debts, and there was a threat of wholesale foreclosures. The cold statistics told the story: In 1932 net farm income was less than one-third what it had been three years before and the rate of parity (the ratio of prices paid to farmers to the prices they are charged for commodities) fell from 89 in 1929 to 55 in 1932. The situation was so desperate that in January, 1933, the head of the Farm Bureau Federation forecast to a Senate committee a "revolution in the countryside" within twelve months unless relief came.

In such emergency circumstances, the President did not hesitate to entertain radical proposals if they showed any promise of improving the

farm situation. Advice came from all directions—from farm organization leaders themselves, farm economists, and from some of the notably
nonagrarian experts of the brains trust. Rex Tugwell, who became
Assistant Secretary of Agriculture saw four general positions taken by
various types of reformers. First, there were those who would simply fix
prices by law or administrative decree; second, others looked abroad and
found the answer to crop surpluses in dumping on the world market;
third, some policy-makers favored marketing agreements to reduce the
overabundance; finally, the solution was seen by still others in reducing
acreage and thus limiting supply.

The Agricultural Adjustment Act, which came out of Congress as
the result of conflicting pressures, provided a number of options for the
Agricultural Administrator and thus did not constitute a policy decision
but rather a grab bag of legal alternatives. In this sense, particularly, it
was a sweeping piece of legislation and was roundly denounced by conservatives, who saw it as "revolutionary," "bolshevist," and, in the words
of Congressman Joseph Martin, a first step on "the road to Moscow."

The possibility of limiting production by paying farmers to participate in production control programs such as acreage allotment reduc-
tions or, alternatively, putting up farm prices by means of marketing
agreements among farmers, processors, and distributors held different
attractions to different people. In an attempt to give the whole Agricultural Adjustment program a cover of conservative legitimacy, FDR
appointed George Peek as Administrator. Peek was a representative of
the old school of McNary Haugenism which saw its mission as a single-
minded devotion to the cause of raising farm prices, regardless of the
effect on the rest of the nation's economy or that of the world. The logic
of the proposition was rather simple. A sound policy, for Peek, was one
which encouraged production at home along with marketing agreements
to push up farm prices. Surpluses were no problem; they would merely
be exported. A two-price system would protect the American farmer's
production by a sufficiently high tariff barrier and a government export
program designed to find foreign markets at any price for excess production.

The administrative problem here is that the ideas of the Administrator of the program were considered antiquated, rustic, economic provincialism by a healthy proportion of his liberal subordinates. These offi-

cials constituted a group of urban intellectuals who were trying to bring about *general* economic reforms in American life. The liberal faction was led by Rexford Tugwell, the Assistant Secretary of Agriculture and Jerome Frank, the General Counsel. The latter, one of the brilliant legal minds of his day, recruited, with the help of Professor Frankfurter, a corps of luminaries from the law firms and professional schools around the country. From Chicago came Adlai Stevenson; from the Yale Law School came Thurman Arnold and Abe Fortas; the Harvard Law School contributed Alger Hiss, Lee Pressman, John Abt, and Nathan Witt. Together they formed a phalanx of opposition to the Administrator and, through Tugwell and Frank, fought for leverage with the Secretary, Henry Wallace, and the President.

The mutual contempt existing between Peek and his staff grew. And since the Administrator was highly conservative and openly anti-intellectual in a regime which thrived on intellectual liberalism, he had just cause to feel beleaguered. For while Peek worked simply to raise farm prices, much of his legal staff was even more concerned to relieve poverty among sharecroppers and tenant farmers and to force economic concessions out of processors and distributors in order that increased farm prices not come out of the pockets of consumers.

Benignly presiding over the skirmishes going on in his Department, Wallace shifted from one side to another on the big conflicts, not being able to accept Peek's agrarian provincialism and, at the same time, not intellectually and temperamentally capable of going all the way with the radical urban intellectuals. At the end of 1933, with Wallace out of Washington, Tugwell was able to bring the conflict to a climax and persuade the President to remove Peek; but this proved to be only a temporary palliative. To replace Peek, Henry Wallace chose Chester Davis, a man of broader social outlook than Peek, but one who refused to tolerate what he saw as insubordination in the enthusiastic reformers of his agency. Hence, almost exactly one year after the victory of the social outlook group in the AAA, Davis demanded and got the resignations of Frank and Pressman, along with others on the second string of the reform team.

While the reorganization of American agriculture under the New Deal laid bare fundamental ideological differences within the Administration, another source of conflict prominently represented in the bureaucracy of the 1930s was the controversy that often rose over emphases, priorities, and choices of time and circumstance in establishing new programs and policies. Thus Hugh Johnson would move too fast for the tastes of some in getting the NRA codes established while Harold Ickes was agonizingly deliberate in the eyes of others in getting public works projects established.

In retrospect a major battle of significance turning on the question of timing was the conflict between economic nationalism and internationalism in the early years of the New Deal. Although the more far-sighted New Dealers, and the President himself, were not committed to a rigid economic nationalism, the logic of internal reform on a broad scale did argue for a minimum of external economic influence. Thus the President, in his first Inaugural Address stated that he would spare no effort to restore world trade, "but the emergency at home cannot wait on that accomplishment."

In the months that followed the inauguration of the New Deal, the hopes of internationalists—and most particularly, those of that dedicated internationalist, Secretary of State Cordell Hull—were to be disappointed by a series of acts which approached economic isolation. The guide to New Deal trade and world monetary policy was given clearly in the ludicrous charade played out at the World Economic Conference.

Even as the new Administration took office, preparations were being made for the Economic Conference which was to take place in London in the midsummer of 1933. In May the President informed Hull that he hoped to see a tariff truce brought about, a coordinated monetary and fiscal policy, removal of foreign exchange restrictions, and gradual reduction of tariff barriers. Thus the Secretary of State left for London with high hopes. The hopes were based not merely upon presidential public pronouncements favoring lower tariffs, but on private presidential promises that the Reciprocal Trade Agreements bill would be submitted to Congress while the London Conference was underway. Hull was thus chagrined to receive cables from Washington, while on shipboard heading for London, outlining new legislation to *raise* tariffs and indications that the reciprocity measure would not be submitted to Congress. Hull cabled the President, pleading for reciprocity and received a crushing reply:

> I wholly understand and approve your anxiety for tariff action at this session. The situation in these closing days of the session is so full of dynamite that immediate adjournment is necessary. Otherwise bonus legislation, paper money inflation, etc., may be forced. . . . Therefore, tariff legislation seems not only highly inadvisable, but impossible of achievement.

For Hull the primary purpose of his attendance at the Conference had been removed. To make matters worse, the American delegation had not been chosen by Hull, but by the President, and included members wholly unsympathetic to tariff reduction, some of whom had other axes to grind. Thus Senator Key Pittman, chief spokesman for domestic silver interests, worked at the Conference to get the United States Government committed to purchasing silver.

As the divided American delegation became an object of derision among foreign observers, President Roosevelt dispatched Raymond Moley to the Conference, encouraging the expectation that Moley would provide leadership for the American delegation and act as a clear representative of the Administration's real position on the great economic issues. On arriving, Moley approved a statement committing the United States to participate in international currency stabilization. Two days later Roosevelt sent what came to be called his "bombshell" message in which he denounced currency stabilization, seeing in it an attempt by world economic powers to interfere with New Deal policies designed to raise prices at home. The President went even further to scold nations who lacked balanced budgets and did not live within their means. The Conference—and, for the time, hopes for international trade and monetary cooperation—was finished.

Back in Washington the claims of the New Deal nationalists continued for some time to take precedence over those of Hull and his internationalist friends. Hugh Johnson, head of the NRA, fought the threat that international influences might hold for the price-fixing operations overseen by his Agency. For Raymond Moley, Hull's internationalism was seen as "threatening the integrity and unity of the New Deal on every side" and, "incompatible with the idea of a managed economy." The cruelest irony of all for Hull, however, was the fact that the President's Special Advisor on Foreign Trade was none other than George Peek. To facilitate easing Peek out of the AAA, Roosevelt had kicked him upstairs to the foreign trade position, knowing well that Peek was a rabid nationalist.

By mid-1934 Cordell Hull's campaign for reciprocity achieved its first important success. He finally succeeded in persuading the President that the time was ripe for the legislative measure. In doing so, Hull was aided by his cabinet colleague, Henry Wallace of the Agriculture Department. Wallace had come out against economic nationalism in an influential pamphlet, *America Must Choose*, written in the spring of 1934.

Furthermore, the President (who, be it remembered, was not personally committed to nationalism in any case) was pressured not only by members of his own Administration, but even by such internationalist Republican luminaries as Henry L. Stimson. In June the Reciprocal Trade Agreements Act was signed by the President and the way was clear for more cooperative trade relations with the rest of the world. The administration of the Act would, of course, be the final test. The anticlimactic event in this story comes at the end of 1935 when, after more than a year's attempt to water down the internationalism of the Act, Peek went a step too far. In a broadside address entitled *America's Choice*, the trade advisor suggested that the policies of the Internationalists were nothing short of un-American and were weakening the nation. Roosevelt fired off a letter to his Administrator denouncing the "silly" tone of the speech. Four days later the President accepted Peek's resignation and the course of American economic policy was further directed toward internationalism.

Differing goals of policy and differing strategies applied for their implementation are common sources of bureaucratic conflict, but the dreamers who conjure up the goals and the planners who develop the strategies are men, so the personal element is necessarily involved. Confusion, conflict, and controversy in the early years of the New Deal were thus at least partly attributable to human foibles in the bureaucratic setting. Status rivalries, personal competitiveness, and personality clashes were not uncommon in a collection of individualists as temperamental as many of the New Dealers. None was a better example of bureaucratic vanity than the Secretary of Interior, Harold L. Ickes.

For years a major source of discomfiture for Secretary Ickes was the organization and administration of federal relief programs. In the spring of 1935 Congress voted generous relief funds amounting to some $4.8 billion. The appropriation resolution left the President complete discretion to set up the relief administration. Immediately Roosevelt was faced with a dilemma. In one sense the ideal candidate to manage the relief program was Harry Hopkins, the Federal Emergency Relief Administrator. On the other hand, Harold Ickes, the careful, absolutely honest Public Works Administrator loomed as a logical policeman over the nearly $5 billion relief operation. Finally, the President decided that the parsimonious Ickes would be in charge of an Allotment Division and the easy-spending Hopkins would take over the projects division. This typical Rooseveltian compromise required an umpire to complete the administrative balancing act. The first choice of the President for intermediary between Ickes and Hopkins was Joseph P. Kennedy who simply refused the job, being disinclined to intrude in that potential hornet's nest. At length Frank Walker, Director of the President's Emergency Council, was given the unenviable task.

From the outset Hopkins was determined not to be bound by the purse-string tugs of the Interior Secretary. He immediately persuaded the President to create out of his meager projects division a Works Projects Administration. The appropriate executive order served to launch Hopkins' imperial relief design much to Ickes's consternation. From the spring of 1935 on, no source serves as a better index to Ickes's progressive rage than the old curmudgeon's own *Diaries*. At first Ickes, feeling the plan for divided authority was patently unworkable, suspected that the President was simply arranging a takeover of the Secretary's Public Works Administration without unduly jarring him.

As time went by, Ickes—assured by the President of his strategic importance to the relief administration—attempted to be a watchdog over Hopkins. In April, 1935 Ickes sensed that Hopkins was "playing up to Walker" in order to undercut any restraining influence—influence that was vital since the WPA Administrator was likely to "fly off on tangents unless he is watched."

By June Ickes referred to Treasury Secretary Morgenthau, an ally of Hopkins, as a "satellite" who had the presumption to intrude in relief meetings. Moreover, matters had reached a stage where Hopkins's WPA and Ickes's PWA were in sharp competition in the relief business, and

Ickes bemoaned the fact that Hopkins wanted "no rules that will prevent his organization from grabbing everything in sight." What Hopkins was grabbing amounted to such things as lump-sum appropriations for his own discretionary projects; the right to pass on Ickes's public works projects; and the public limelight in the relief field.

By the end of August Ickes was thoroughly convinced that he was the object of a conspiracy. Remorsefully he tells himself that long hours and hard work are rewarding:

> But I don't take naturally to fighting such underhand efforts as Morgenthau and Hopkins have been putting in to undermine me and aggrandize themselves. The President certainly has a blind side so far as Morgenthau is concerned, and Hopkins seems to sing a siren song for him.

Hopkins, for his part, looked upon Ickes as a crotchety bore and contributed at least an equal share to the feud. The President attempted to patch the relations up between his surly subordinates, but to little avail. For, fundamentally, as Sherwood has suggested, the difference between them was largely one of personality. Hopkins was a welfare worker trying to relieve the suffering he saw about him with little concern for administrative or financial niceties. Ickes, on the other hand, was basically a businessman, though certainly a liberal one. For the Secretary, suffering was a more abstract condition, to be treated, yes, but with cautious, businesslike measures.

Many an administrative problem originates not in philosophical antipathy, competition among strategies, or personal rivalries, but merely in organizational dysfunctions common to large institutions. It was not surprising that some organizational problems in the New Deal bureaucracy were caused by the rapid growth of the governmental machine. In 1936, the President's Committee on Administrative Management, headed by Louis Brownlow, took a close look at the bureaucracy. It noted that the civilian employees of the executive branch had grown from 578,231 in 1932 to 824,259 in 1936 and that there were more than 100 separately organized establishments and agencies reporting to the President. The Committee concluded that it was impossible to have a rational exercise of control over such a far-flung empire and that a re-grouping and consolidation of functions was imperative.

Overlapping functions and responsibilities caused a particular debility in administration. The PWA and the WPA illustrate this point. Even after Hopkins's WPA came to dominate the relief field, its projects involved relationships with other federal agencies in at least three different ways. WPA had relationships with other agencies operating other relief functions, such as the Farm Security Agency. It also had relationships with agencies that provided it with technical assistance, such as the Public Health Service or the Civil Aeronautics Authority. Finally, there were relationships with such agencies as the Treasury Department and the Employees' Compensation Commission which performed services for the WPA.

At other times problems of inter-program conflict developed as the activities of one agency impeded or burdened the mission of another agency. In the February 20, 1934, meeting of the National Emergency Council, the Secretary of Labor, Frances Perkins, interrupted the report of the Agricultural Adjustment Administrator, Chester Davis, to ask about the effects of acreage reduction. Miss Perkins was disturbed about the temporary dislocation of tenant farmers as a result of the cutback in farm production. The Federal Emergency Relief Administrator, Harry Hopkins, noted that plowing under cotton in certain southern districts had displaced thousands of people who were absorbed on the relief rolls. Hopkins lamented that his relief administrators forecast tens of thousands of additional cases on relief as a result of the cotton program alone.

The implementation of decisions and policies is particularly difficult in an organization so distended that the assurance of compliance is nearly unattainable. From the top down, the problem is the same: how to assure that authoritative commands will be heeded? Modern bureaucracy is based on a hierarchical organization wherein each level of the organization receives orders from the level above it and duly implements these directives. In practice, accountability is not nearly so easily guaranteed. Roosevelt himself was unable to enforce a continuous adherence to his wishes as he admitted in an outburst memorable for its exasperated candor:

The Treasury is so large and far-flung and ingrained in its practices that I find it almost impossible to get the action and results I want—even with Henry [Morgenthau] there. But the Treasury is not to be compared with the State Department. You should go through the experience of trying to get any changes in the thinking, policy, and action of the career diplomats and then you'd know what a real problem was. But the Treasury and the State Department put together are nothing as compared with the Na-a-vy. The admirals are really something to cope with—and I should know. To change anything in the Na-a-vy is like punching a feather bed. You punch it with your right and you punch it with your left until you are finally exhausted, and then you find the damn bed just as it was before you started punching.

Not only the President but also his subordinates were subject to the same frustrations. A careful study of the WPA relates how the Washington headquarters worked out an apparently rational formula for judging the size of the state offices and the appropriate budgets for their operations. In practice, there was a general tendency to exceed the prescribed staff level. This was done without qualms since the whole operation was so complicated that original guidelines seemed irrelevant to local situations. The result was that "although not formally rescinded, the original limits on size of administrative personnel were simply ignored in practice."

ROOSEVELT AS ADMINISTRATIVE LEADER

Because of the wide publicity given to incidents and problems such as those considered in the preceding section, it was long a fashion of New Deal criticism—even among political and temperamental allies of the movement—to decry the "sloppy administration" which characterized it. More recent studies of the period, however, have called this easy judgment into question. Let us suppose that four criteria for analyzing this kind of leadership grow out of the four problem areas considered in the last few pages. That is, the exercise of administrative leadership requires that attention be given to (1) the establishment of policy goals; (2) the method of implementing these goals—strategy, timing, and choices among priorities; (3) the use of personnel in implementing policy; and (4) the organizational problem of fashioning a structural framework which enhances rational decision-making and execution.

In the sense that a superior administrative chief should have in mind a precise framework and a detailed catalogue of goals which he can set before his subordinates with a call for implementation, Roosevelt was a weak administrative leader. It is clear that the President did not have a clear blueprint for action in each area—business, agriculture, labor, public finance, welfare and the rest—in March, 1933. To be sure he had some ideas about each of these problem areas (the balanced budget, for example, seemed almost to be enshrouded in sanctity) but he was prepared to be flexible, to learn, to experiment. Thus he could tolerate the situation described in the Agriculture Department until he was convinced that the conservative head of the AAA was further from the correct orientation in farm policy than those who opposed him.

Another example of Rooseveltian open-mindedness (which many financial titans considered evil-mindedness and some economists considered empty-mindedness) was the short-lived experiment in gold buying. The shame of this venture was not that it was particularly harmful, but that in it the President was temporarily captivated by an exotic scheme proffered by one of his advisors to the exclusion of alternative suggestions by others.

Still another ambiguity in the thinking of the Administration was the sharp cleavage between the intellectual followers of Brandeis and those brains trusters who favored a partnership with big business. From the outset the President appeared to accept the views of Moley and Tugwell which eventuated in the National Industrial Recovery Act. The result of that Act was the establishment of hundreds of codes governing the relations between capital and labor and establishing standards of "fair" competition in industry. The government played a key role in drawing up and, in some cases, even imposing the codes. The great good which resulted from these codes, with their symbolic stamp of public legitimacy—the Blue Eagle—was the atmosphere or popular myth of general recovery which they fostered. Unfortunately, the NRA was less effective in producing real recovery and came to be heavily influenced by big business. As a result of damaging evidence brought to light by the special Darrow Committee, established to investigate the NRA, Roosevelt was prepared to see it—and the concept of a business-government partnership—pass from the scene. After NRA's official burial by the Supreme Court in 1935, business policy took on a much more Brandeisian hue as the Justice Department began vigorous antitrust activity and as the atomization formula was resuscitated. Such a turnabout brought disillusionment to those like Moley, Tugwell, and Johnson, who were much more intellectually committed to a precise goal of policy than was the President.

Can we conclude then, that Roosevelt really had no convictions about policy, that he was a complete pragmatist, willing to try any line of attack or even nostrum, as long as it achieved some salutary results or until it proved hopeless or politically unpopular? There is much evidence to indicate that such a characterization regarding *specific* policies is not grossly wide of the mark. And yet, one wonders how exacting the goals of the good administrator must be. For if we are to concede that there existed for Roosevelt a set of fairly consistent, broad goals based on a perceptive understanding of his environment, and formed in the context of a traditional American mentality, then we may revise our estimate.

I would argue that such a revision is needed. Roosevelt recognized a fact of first importance in that America had become a modern, urban, industrialized, interdependent mass society. In the 1960s that statement is a cliché; it was not so in the 1930s. The much more comfortable and orthodox image of society dated from the nineteenth century. Moreover, Roosevelt's understanding of his society led him to certain operative conclusions which were embodied in his leadership. Among them was the intellectual acceptance of positive government, of the need for political centralization. The ravages of a mass depression led him to accept also the need for mass public welfare. Add to these understandings and convictions a basically democratic and liberal orientation and a shrewd sense of the imperatives of pluralism in American politics, and there is a strong case for the presence of a basic direction, a set of basic guiding principles of administrative leadership.

Finally, it has been stated that the hallmark of creative leadership is that influence which gets beyond administrative management to institutional innovation and change. To the extent, then, that Franklin Roosevelt's predispositions and activities led directly to the popular legitimacy of a centralized government underwriting a welfare state and regulating a wide sector of the economy, he reshaped the office of the presidency and bequeathed to his successors an expanded corpus of administrative expectations and even demands.

Franklin Roosevelt's administrative strategy was directed to one central purpose: the maintenance of ultimate, personal control. It is ironic that one of the chief criticisms of his administration is that the means by which he held the reins gave the appearance not of management and control, but of confusion, uncertainty, and an absence of accountability. Roosevelt's brand of management was misunderstood because he did not follow the scholastic maxims of administrative supervision. For example, the New Deal administrations were characterized not by clear, symmetrical divisions of functions and allocations of responsibility and authority; rather, as Schlesinger has so acutely described the Roosevelt style:

> His favorite technique was to keep grants of authority incomplete, jurisdictions uncertain, charters overlapping. The result of this competitive theory of administration was often confusion and exasperation on the operating level; but no other method could so reliably insure that in a large bureaucracy filled with ambitious men eager for power the decisions, and the power to make them, would remain with the President.

Thus FDR decided it would be wise to appoint separate administrators for each of the two major titles of the National Industrial Recovery Act. He placed Hugh Johnson in charge of Title I (industrial codes and labor) and Harold Ickes in charge of Title II (public works). Johnson was purple with consternation at the arrangement, and in the months that followed there was friction between Johnson and Ickes, two individualists of the first order. But the President got exactly what he wanted: vigorous application in the process of drawing up industrial codes from General Johnson and careful, scrupulous, absolutely honest oversight in public works expenditures from Ickes.

This pattern would repeat itself again and again in the New Deal era. Later the responsibility for public works and relief projects would be divided between Ickes and Harry Hopkins, raising the blood pressure of both, but serving as an internal goad and counter-checking arrangement for each. The same model served the Securities Exchange Commission, where Kennedy as Chairman provided the appropriate background for the job and a sincere and hard-working earnestness in its accomplishment but was helped along with the technical expertise of James Landis and Ferdinand Pecora. In a political sense, as well, the presence of Landis and Pecora on the Commission served to neutralize the charge that FDR had put his major financial policing device in the hands of a reactionary Wall Street financier.

There is a further importance in these arrangements which goes to the heart of his method of presidential control. By having different agencies (such as PWA and WPA) operating in the same area or divided authority within an agency (SEC, NRA, etc.), Roosevelt provided both a method of controlling—*dividere et imperare*—and a source of options in the event of trouble. Hence with a shift in personnel (Ickes to Hopkins; Johnson to Richberg; Kennedy to Landis) or a shift in emphasis on the mission of one agency to another, the President could more easily make such departures in policy orientation as events suggested. As Frances Perkins—one of the most intimate and long-term associates of the President—noted in her recollections: "He was a great believer in alternatives. He rarely got himself sewed tight to a program from which there was no turning back."

Timing is a vital aspect of administrative leadership. The noblest of quests, if presented at the wrong time, may founder in the face of lesser claims to attention that have already been asserted. Roosevelt sensed this principle and usually managed his subordinates and their demands in a way that permitted him maximum flexibility in setting a new course or altering an old one, pursuing a new policy or disposing of an old one. In the process, of course, he aroused the wrath of many of his aides and confidants, but more often than not he succeeded in granting himself the needed room in which to maneuver. As Richard Neustadt has written, FDR was a master at setting his own deadlines—and meeting them.

In November, 1934, the people seemed to give the New Deal a resounding vote of confidence in the congressional elections. Yet in the months that followed, very little happened. The new Congress passed only one important piece of legislation in the spring of 1935, and little direction emanated from the White House. Political friends of the President complained, both privately in letters and personal meetings and publicly in the press and magazines, about the absence of leadership and disheartening delays in the reform program. Clearly Roosevelt was having some reservations about the direction in which his New Deal was heading and refused to be hurried along. Then on May 27 the Supreme Court in the *Schecter* case declared the NRA unconstitutional. On the same day ("Black Monday") the Court also struck down the New Deal relief act for farm mortgagors and further restricted the President's power of removal of administrators.

In the days that followed, Roosevelt made up his mind about the future course of his New Deal. What historians have come to refer to as the "Second New Deal" took shape in May-June, 1935. Immediately after the *Schecter* decision, the President called together first his cabinet and then a congressional leadership conference and announced a full-speed-ahead campaign for major legislation. He presented a "must" list which included the Social Security Bill, the Wagner Labor Bill, a banking bill, a public utility holding company bill, and a progressive tax ("soak the rich") bill. Before the end of August Congress had passed all the "must" bills, making 1935 the most momentous legislative year in the New Deal in a long-term sense. On the heels of adversity, Roosevelt had seized the initiative and set out on a new course marked by more welfare and insurance schemes of a permanent rather than an emergency nature, more regulatory activity, and less comprehensive national planning.

Any President is a prisoner of the information available to him. Moreover, not only the substantive details of economics and social reality, but also the knowledge of what is going on in his own administrative household is indispensable to an effective leader. Franklin Roosevelt was shrewdly adept at collecting such information. This too was sometimes a source of pique and internal conflict among the New Dealers who were subject to some of the President's devious methods of learning what was going on. One habit FDR indulged was the practice of talking to lower level subordinates in the bureaucracy without passing through the normal channels of the cabinet head or agency supervisor. Beyond this, many of the President's informants originated outside the public bureaucracy. Grace Tully, long a presidential secretary, relates how the President often used Sam Rosenman to check out information and how he would also give the same assignment to Congressman James

Byrnes. Sometimes the checkers would encounter each other checking the identical information which created, in Mrs. Tully's words, "ruffled feathers" but which served the President's purpose.

In seeking out his information the President cultivated accuracy in his informants by creating the impression that stories should not be merely accepted at face value. A former aide of the President described the routine to Richard Neustadt as follows:

> He would call you in and ask you to get the story on some complicated business, and you'd come back after a couple of days of hard labor and present the juicy morsel you'd uncovered under a stone somewhere, and *then* you'd find out he knew all about it, along with something else you *didn't* know. Where he got his information from he wouldn't mention, usually, but after he had done this to you once or twice you got damn careful about *your* information.

The strategy Roosevelt used to organize events is inseparable from his method of handling people, for much of the former depended on the latter. The essence of Roosevelt's administrative style was personal. He seemed most assured and most effective when performing as the intuitive psychologist he was.

The profusion of papers, journals, diaries, memoirs, books, and articles which FDR's aides and confidants have produced testifies (in some cases, unintentionally) to the Chief's skill at manipulation. Understanding the extreme vanity of some of the people he had collected in his entourage, Roosevelt could be a consummate flatterer when the occasion called for it. The President would ignore the requests and even the presence of the hapless Ickes for months and even break promises solemnly made to the Secretary. And then, when the crises came, usually in the form of a letter of resignation, Roosevelt would either face the ruffled Ickes personally with a manner of mock regret or even penitence, or write a cleverly phrased note suggesting that the Secretary and the President really saw eye to eye and that the former's continued presence in the administration was indispensable. On one such occasion Ickes mused to himself, after reading the Rooseveltian *billet-doux*: "I read this communication and was quite touched by its undoubted generosity and its evident sincerity of tone."

Frances Perkins, the Secretary of Labor (and not a professional resigner) relates in *The Roosevelt I Knew* a similar incident that illustrates just how accurate Roosevelt's sense of the appropriate line of argument was:

> Once when I was trying to resign, he wrinkled up his nose in the way he sometimes did when he was trying to be funny and said, "Well, I don't think it would be so good politically. I notice we haven't lost the labor vote or the women's vote on your account."

And then, Miss Perkins goes on, with an interpretation that speaks worlds for Roosevelt's ability to touch the right chord:

> As a matter of fact, the votes in these two fields had greatly increased in the years of the New Deal. It was characteristic of him that he had noticed those things and had realized that, however much of a pain I might be to some people, the majority of the voters had not reacted unfavorably to my programs.

Just as Roosevelt intentionally cultivated competition among different agencies in the same field of policy, he encouraged rivalry among his subordinates. Social invitations, telephone chats, and whispered conferences were often conducted with a flair of publicity that aroused the curiosity and envy of those not being favored by presidential attention at the moment. Cabinet members have noted that much of the serious work was done *after* the formal cabinet meeting in private conferences with the President. Roosevelt preferred it that way, for it permitted him greater flexibility and sometimes, even the opportunity for duplicity. He once confided to his Secretary of Labor: "A little rivalry is stimulating you know. It keeps everybody going to prove that he is a better fellow than the next. It keeps them honest too."

All these techniques and many more were applied by the President in getting the maximum of both efficiency and accountability out of his aides. Nonetheless, it would be misleading to suggest that FDR was not dependent upon his subordinates simply because he used them skillfully. And this dependence can be the beginning of dominance over any president who is not constantly aware of the threat to his administrative integrity. Roosevelt guarded against this threat primarily by maintaining a bureaucratic pluralism constructed out of a continuous circulation of the elite of administrative functionaries. To be sure, there was always a palace guard, or a "Janissariat" as Hugh Johnson thought of it; but faces changed frequently. The press had a field day attempting to pick the "Number One Man" or the clique which allegedly had the President's ear. Yet, as time went by, an honest observer had to admit that, though Professor Moley seemed on top at the outset, that Henry Morgenthau was thought to spend as much time in the Presidential Office as the President, that Professor Frankfurter's "boys" (Corcoran, Cohen, Frank, *et al.*) ran the New Deal, each individual and group would be eclipsed by another in a relatively short time.

A final consideration should be entered concerning Roosevelt's relations with his subordinates. It has been commonly charged that FDR was weak when it came to disciplining his subordinates and incapable of discharging an aide, even for acts of disloyalty to the administration or the President. If a narrow definition of dismissal is adopted, perhaps there is something to this observation. However, a more meaningful understanding of Roosevelt's control is achieved if we realize that a presidential acceptance of a resignation is just as effective as a formal removal. In this context, there are endless examples where a presidential shift in policy, subtle acts of presidential hostility, or a presidential reorganization of authorities and responsibilities would leave the individual affected no alternative but to resign. Moley, Peek, Johnson, Richberg, Lewis Douglas, Jones, Hopkins, and many others could give personal testimony to this truth.

Since administration is a product of institutional structure as well as personal function, there remains to be considered the question of FDR's performance of organizational responsibilities. The fundamental test of the quality of this stewardship is simply: Did the President influence the institutional framework of executive power for better or for worse?

Roosevelt's approach to the problem of structural organization seems to have been that of one who engages unenthusiastically in a necessary confrontation with bothersome details because of the realization that they symbolize more important principles. FDR found no joy in contemplating the pictorial neatness of organization charts; to the extent that he concerned himself with them at all, it was because he was convinced that here was one additional aspect of the husbandry he practiced with his own power. In short, he understood that he could not handle all the problems personally (much as he would have liked to!) that would develop in such a large bureaucratic establishment.

His first response—and one which continued throughout his administrations—was simply to create new operating agencies to perform the functions his New Deal created. This was not done out of a personal thirst for additional executive appointments or an intellectual fetish for ever-expanding bureaucracy. Rather, the boards, agencies, commissions, administrations, authorities, and corporations which flourished in alphabetical profusion in the 1930s were grounded on an entirely logical principle: the integrity of the fresh start. As FDR stated it himself,

> Why not establish a new agency to take over the new duty rather than saddle it on an old institution? Of course, a great many mistakes are going to be made. . . . We have to be prepared to absorb and correct them quickly. We have to be prepared to abandon bad practices that grow up out of ignorance. It seems to me it is easier to use a new agency which is not a permanent part of the structure of government. If it is not permanent, we don't get bad precedents. . . . We can do anything that needs to be done and then discard the agency when the emergency is over.

Roosevelt early realized that coordination of the activities of the far-flung agencies of the bureaucracy was needed. His first attempt at coordination—the Executive Council—gave way in November, 1933, to the more enduring National Emergency Council. The NEC was a group of shifting membership made up of cabinet and leading agency supervisors organized to deal in a collective way with all the problems related to recovery. As a coordinating agency, NEC was not very successful beyond bringing to the attention of those who attended its sessions what was happening in other departments. Even in this connection, the value of the meetings was limited because various agencies distributed long mimeographed reports on their activities to the conferees who simply did not have time to read them carefully, if at all.

Nevertheless, the NEC performed two valuable functions. First, it gave the President a lecture platform wider than the cabinet from which to educate the leading members of his Administration. In fact, this is the dominant theme which constantly reasserts itself as one reads though the transcripts of the NEC *Proceedings*. At one point the President counsels his aides about the importance of their activities in the eyes of the public and admonishes them to develop a public relations sense. At another point, he warns them quite sternly, complete with the use of a bad example afforded by an erring colleague, against treating congressmen cavalierly or impolitely. And at another meeting he lectures about interagency lobbying and the dangers inherent in one administrator's commenting on the work of another's agency in the atmosphere of a press conference.

The second important dividend of the NEC meetings was the establishment of a system of legislative clearance. In December, 1934, the President established the rule that, henceforth, departmental and agency requests for legislation were not to be made directly in testimony before Congress but were to be cleared through the Executive Director of the NEC (then Donald Richberg) and the President himself. When the Secretary of Labor protested that it was very difficult to avoid appearances before congressional committees requested on short notice and that the administrator could not make excuses forever, the President replied: "And before you appear, come and talk to Papa."

The enduring value in Roosevelt's NEC clearance notion is that even after NEC fell into disuse, the clearance function was absorbed by the Bureau of the Budget and has become an important tool of coordination for presidents in protecting their freedom of choice over policy alternatives and, thus, their administrative leadership.

The crowning achievement of administrative reorganization in the New Deal era was undoubtedly the creation of the Executive Office of the President. Indeed, Clinton Rossiter has concluded about the view that FDR was a "second-rate administrator" that: "In light of Executive Order 8248, an accomplishment in public administration superior to that of any other President, this familiar judgment seems a trifle musty." In 1936 Roosevelt had established a Committee on Administrative Management which, after months of research into the federal bureaucracy, concluded that the President needed help. In response Congress legislated reorganization authority for the President and Roosevelt made sure use of that discretion to create the Executive Office.

The new device served and continues to serve the function of providing yet another source of information for the President; of assuring that matters requiring his attention reach his desk promptly; of further centralizing and coordinating the execution of national policy; and of providing the President additional controls over the activities of his subordinates. The immediate transfer of the Bureau of the Budget from the Treasury Department to the Executive Office, brought within the intimacy of the White House the central clearance mechanism Roosevelt had established a few years earlier. Furthermore, in later years the Executive Office has come to embody national economic planning, national security policy making, research and development in space, and the coordination of international trade negotiations.

CONCLUSION

Final judgments on the performance of a complex set of tasks carried out over a period of years are notably difficult to make and are often so balanced as to be totally equivocal. Yet the judgments must be made, if only to stimulate further investigation into the questions. Drawing from both the characteristics of administrative leadership and the barriers to that leadership suggested here, the conclusion is a clear affirmation of Franklin Roosevelt's ability at the job.

The weaknesses were clear and public. Roosevelt courted controversy. He permitted, even seemed to encourage excessive duplication and open conflict among his subordinates. Sometimes the direction of his administration was in doubt. In the process, the public image of some members of the official family was less than distinguished; money was undoubtedly wasted; and other economies of time and energy and intellect were sacrificed.

But the public weaknesses were often obscured and more than compensated by private executive strengths. Chief among these strengths was the ability to seek out, organize, and effectively use human material. Hardly of secondary importance was the atmosphere of receptivity to new ideas and a willingness to experiment. That this is not the characteristic atmosphere of bureaucracy is perhaps what makes it so attractive in retrospect.

In any case, given the overburdening challenges thrown down by the depression years, the response made by Franklin Roosevelt as administrative leader was impressive. Several years ago, Harold Smith, a former Budget Director and typically traditional, cautious administrator, concluded on the basis of a long period of service under FDR:

> I think I'd say that Roosevelt must have been one of the greatest geniuses as an administrator that ever lived. What we couldn't appreciate at the time was the fact that he was a real *artist* in government.

CHARLES E. JACOB

Vassar College

part one

THE
BRAINS
TRUST

We are so accustomed to the presence of academic experts filling important roles at the summit of political power that it may seem surprising that the overt presence of the professors, particularly at the outset, provided a source of controversy for the New Deal. That assemblage of brains trusters marks one of Roosevelt's unique stylistic contributions to government personnel administration. The descriptive chapter printed here comes from a book written hurriedly in 1933 by a leading journalist who had "covered" FDR since his election to the New York governorship in 1929. Lindley's sketches are interesting period pieces about some of the leading thinkers and the backgrounds, qualities, and attitudes they brought to Washington of the early 1930s. Lindley —himself an intellectual sympathetic to the "Roosevelt Revolution"— transmits some of that atmosphere of enthusiasm which marked the period.

The Roosevelt Revolution

Ernest K. Lindley

Raymond Moley's resignation as Assistant Secretary of State in September 1933 provoked speculative furore of an intensity theretofore reserved for such notable disruptions in the government as William Jennings Bryan's retirement from President Wilson's Cabinet. Conservatives of various stripes gleefully proclaimed the disintegration of the celebrated brains trust and hopefully forecast a retreat from the innovations of the New Deal toward the traditional thought of the Democratic party. Liberals tried to reassure themselves that Mr. Moley's resignation portended no change in the major trends of President Roosevelt's policies. In the excitement one significant occurrence was generally overlooked. The day before Mr. Moley's resignation was announced, Mr. Roosevelt made a speech in Poughkeepsie in which he reiterated that the major objectives of the experimental ventures of the New Deal were the permanent objectives of his Administration.

No aspect of the New Deal has been subjected to hotter attack and defense than the brains trust. As hammer blows rained on the old regime, conservatives in Congress and the press railed against "theorists" in government and professorial advisers. That was politer and safer than railing against an extremely popular President, and it was undoubtedly true that college professors and other intellectuals had an important hand in the drafting and directing of most of the revolutionary undertakings of the new regime. The renown of the brains trust and of Moley, Tugwell,

Ernest K. Lindley, *The Roosevelt Revolution—First Phase* (New York: The Viking Press, Inc., 1933), pp. 296-315. *Reprinted by permission.*

and Berle spread round the world. Newspaper correspondents began to
examine sedulously each new arrival in Washington to discover if he had
ever taught in a university, possessed a Ph.D degree, or, by aptitude for
making charts or writing treatises, could qualify as a person of unusual
academic attainment. Within a few weeks they had rounded up thirty
or more persons who had one or more of the proper credentials. But they
could never agree on which of them really belonged to the brains trust.
Some preferred to include only those who had taught in universities.
Some preferred to include only the men who saw Mr. Roosevelt frequently, which greatly shortened the list. Others preferred to list all
economists. Still others preferred to make youth the test. Some discrimi-
natingly limited the brains trust to the key people of marked intellectual
capacity and advanced social point of view, a procedure which enabled
them to include a few members of the Cabinet. All of this hubbub and
the position of Professor Moley as one of Mr. Roosevelt's chief advisers
and lieutenants undoubtedly created the picture of a government run by
college professors and economists. To conservatives and liberals alike the
brains trust became the symbol of the economic philosophy embodied in
the experiments of the New Deal. As a matter of fact, by the time the
brains trust received wide publicity it had ceased to exist as an institution.

In the pre-convention campaign of 1932, the brains trust was a definite group. It remained more or less cohesive up to the time of
Mr. Roosevelt's inauguration. Then, in the popular mind, the experts
for the international economic conversations began to be identified as
members of the brains trust. They included three members of the
original brains trust—Moley, Tugwell, and Taussig—and a few of the
newer recruits had access to the President, but there was no longer a
definite body which could be called the brains trust. There were, instead,
various subsidiary brains trusts and many scattered men doing their own
particular jobs. Mr. Moley remained at the President's hand, but the
old round-table discussions practically disappeared. Nevertheless, the
original brains trust was in many respects a unique institution. And,
accepting the brains trust in its general popular sense, the large number
of social scientists that Mr. Roosevelt brought into the government was
a remarkable phenomenon.

In the waves of attack which fell on Raymond Moley during his meteoric career in public life, he was accused in one breath of being a dangerous theorist and in the next of being a mediocre man who had made no mark in the academic world by original contribution to thought. Mr. Moley has an ingenious mind but he probably never will create a doctrine, for he is as hardhearted a realist as Mr. Roosevelt himself.

His early career gave no indication that, when the United States embarked on an audacious experiment at a critical point in the world's history, he would be identified as "the second strongest man in Washington." Of French and Irish descent, he was born in an ordinary American home in Berea, Ohio, near Cleveland, in 1887. He was precocious: at 7 he was reading *Ivanhoe*. At 19 he graduated from obscure Baldwin-Wallace College in Berea and went to the neighboring village of Olmstead Falls as Superintendent of Schools. At 21 he was elected mayor of the village. Bad health sent him West for two years. He returned to teach history in a Cleveland high school and obtain his master's degree from Oberlin. He moved up to Western Reserve University, where he attracted attention locally by requiring his classes to read *The New Republic*. In 1919 he resigned his professorship to take charge of the Cleveland Foundation and make a survey of the causes of organized crime and the breakdown of law enforcement. His findings led to reforms in Cleveland and won discerning praise. He was called upon for similar surveys in Missouri, Illinois, Virginia, Pennsylvania, Connecticut, California, and Indiana. In 1923 he moved to Columbia, where he had received his Ph.D. degree five years earlier, as Associate Professor of Government. The New York State Crime Commission engaged him as an assistant. In 1928 Columbia made him a full Professor of Public Law. He acquired the unusual distinction of being a member of three faculties: the graduate school, the school of law, and Barnard College. At Barnard, his informal lectures and tea-parties became popular.

As literary secretary and dean of the brains trust, Professor Moley was with Mr. Roosevelt during most of the presidential campaign. When Mr. Roosevelt made a trip, Mr. Moley went along with suitcases filled with books and memoranda. After election he went back to his classes at Columbia. Then suddenly in mid-November, newspaper editors began searching furiously for information about him. Mr. Roosevelt had just announced that Mr. Moley would be his sole companion on his visit to the White House to discuss war debts and other world affairs with President Hoover. The announcement fell like a bombshell on important institutions in Wall Street. Private investigation confirmed their worst fears. As a realist he might (and did) realize that the war debt problem had to be dealt with, but his understanding of economics did not coincide with that of our best advertised thinkers. About that time a prominent lady telephoned Mr. Moley to congratulate him on his sudden accession to fame and influence and to rejoice with him that the war debts were about to be canceled. She had an idea for making the process of cancellation so complicated that it would be invisible to the great masses of the people. After talking to her awhile, Professor Moley had one of his periodical explosions. "Madam, I don't know what you are, but I am an American citizen," he said, and hung up the receiver.

With the return from Europe of Norman H. Davis and the drive from Wall Street to wedge him into Mr. Roosevelt's inner circle the attacks on Moley were redoubled. In some of the journals responsive to the financial center one read repeatedly that Mr. Davis had replaced Mr. Moley as Mr. Roosevelt's chief consultant. The record of Mr. Moley's writings and verbal utterances was raked for damaging material, but with very little result. He had never said anything very radical or very startling. Mr. Davis's reports on the current state of Europe and especially his knowledge of the disarmament problem were welcomed by Mr. Roosevelt. But Professor Moley, ably abetted by Dr. Tugwell, remained in full charge of the preparations for the economic conference, and the war debt problem remained securely in the control of Mr. Roosevelt and Mr. Moley.

During the interregnum nobody was busier than Professor Moley in preparing for the launching of the new régime. When the new administration moved in, he was established in the State Department, in quarters conveniently near the White House executive offices. Early every morning he was at the White House for a bedside conference with the President. During the day he was back and forth between the White House and State Department half a dozen times. At night his quarters in the Carlton Hotel were besieged. There were few important laws, few important policies adopted, to which he did not contribute a hand or a word. Meanwhile he bore the main brunt of the work of preparing for the conversations with visiting statesmen and the World Economic Conference. Yet, throughout the exhausting turmoil of those spring months, he continued to return to New York every Thursday to lecture to his classes at Barnard. A visiting British statesman, a firm believer in the virtues of the long British week-end, was aghast at Moley's pace. Mr. Moley explained: "I know of no scientific proof that all work and no play makes Jack a dull boy."

In Washington, Mr. Moley sought the companionship of practical politicians as much as of his old freinds in the brains trust. He did not like to be called "Professor" and he was quick to insist that there was no longer a brains trust. "I have a job and am trying to do it," he asserted stoutly. To accusations that he was a theorist he could reply: "I am essentially a conservative fellow," or "I tilt at no windmills." He professed keen admiration for such practical politicians as James A. Farley, Edward J. Flynn, and Senator Joseph T. Robinson.

"Practical politics is dependent upon ability to guess accurately which way to act," Mr. Moley once said. And it was easy to see in Washington that he was attempting to assess the intangibles of practical politics as accurately as the cold facts of economics. Mr. Moley, however, was no match for the incomparable Mr. Roosevelt as a politician and divining rod of public psychology. And while Mr. Roosevelt's temperamental equipment for the strain of public life is miraculously good, Mr. Moley's is extraordinarily bad. Mr. Moley's quiet drawl and dry humor hint at a serene person. At many critical moments he was a firm sedative for excited colleagues. In his earler days he said that social workers made him weary "because they have no sense of humor." But Moley's usually calm exterior is only a thin crust over a volcano. He explodes frequently. In his Cleveland days two hold-up men pointing revolvers at him made him so angry that he beat them up. In Washington he often seemed on the verge of meting out the same treatment to his adversaries in argument. When he had several days without face-to-face explosion, he exploded in the privacy of his office to his secretaries. Sensitive and intense, he became extremely unhappy under a fierce critical battering. Lacking the craftiness of men more skilled in political warfare, he plunged along boldly, even recklessly, to the July morning that he found himself hailed as "the first casualty" of the new régime.

An explosion in the State Department seemed inevitable from the moment that Cordell Hull and Raymond Moley were put under the same roof. The career diplomats and the political appointees normally keep that department split into two camps. Into that hotbed was thrust Mr. Moley, who was neither a diplomat nor a politician. He might have been put on the payroll of the Treasury Department or almost anywhere else within easy distance of the White House. His job was to assist the President. The State Department was conveniently located and it was an appropriate place for him because he was in charge of preparations for the war debt discussions and the World Economic Conference. Mr. Moley sensed that his position would be embarrassing. He asked that his appointment as Assistant Secretary of State be announced as only temporary. When he was overruled, he asked newspapermen as a personal favor to say that he was to occupy the office only a few weeks.

If Raymond Moley had been possessed of any political wiles, he would have found a way to avoid going to the London Conference. The spectacle was much more amusing at a distance. It was zeal rather than ambition or vanity which took him to London. It was zeal for the Roosevelt Revolution and the policies which Mr. Roosevelt wanted to have advanced at London and too much faith in his enemies—which led him to the unpardonable indiscretion of committing to a cablegram a frank analysis of the delegation.

When he returned, the idea that he was in disgrace was enthusiastically exploited by all who were looking for his scalp. And that was an astonishingly large group of people, including several persons who had close contacts with the President, a large number of conservative Democrats, various miscellaneous individuals, and most of the vested interests in the country. At first there were some external signs of coolness around the White House. But Mr. Moley was soon a daily visitor again. There was plenty of important work for him to do outside the State Department, where he had never handled anything outside the economic field.

Then the plans for a weekly liberal magazine of popular appeal which Mr. Roosevelt and some of his friends had long been brewing suddenly came to a head. As the most publicized intellectual of the New Deal, Mr. Moley was the obvious man to edit this publication. And Vincent Astor, and his co-backers, W. Averell Harriman and Mrs. Mary Rumsey, were willing to pay him a fat salary to do it.

The Administration lost a modern Jacksonian liberal, a sturdy nationalist, and a man who never forgot the public interest. Mr. Moley, one suspects, was inwardly relieved to get out of a maelstrom of intrigue and assault and into a position in which he could express his honest views without worrying about the personal or political consequences.

Rexford G. Tugwell is the philosopher, the sociologist, and the prophet of the Roosevelt Revolution, as well as one of its boldest practitioners. He has provided the movement with much of its rationale (to use one of his favorite words). His broad picture of the whole scope of the American experiment is unmarred by the tough realities of politics. He knows it and it does not perturb him. He makes no pretense of being a practical politician, and one senses that he would prefer never to be known as a politician. While his more sensitive colleague, Mr. Moley strove to dissipate the idea that there was a brains trust, Dr. Tugwell was obviously glad that there had been a brains trust and was sorry that it was not a permanent institution. While Mr. Moley's secretaries spoke of "Mr." Moley, Dr. Tugwell's speak of "Dr." Tugwell. The degree in both cases is Ph.D. Dr. Tugwell believes that economists are needed to plot the course of the modern world and that the politicians' highest duty is to put their ideas into effect. Dr. Tugwell is usually quite a distance ahead of Mr. Roosevelt in his exploration of the potentialities of the new régime. In the vicinity of the White House he is affectionately known as a "Bolshevik." In 1932 it seemed very unlikely that the United States would ever be anything like what Dr. Tugwell thought it should be, but the rapid movements of 1933 began to establish his place as a prophet. The country will probably never catch up with him, for as soon as Dr. Tugwell gets his bearings on a new set of realities he projects lines farther into the future. Forty-two, handsome, poised, he has enjoyed himself to the utmost in Washington, for even in the thick of action he has never lost the calm aloofness of an observer.

Dr. Tugwell was born in Sinclairville in the fruit-raising district of western New York. His father owned a cannery and a farm, but Dr. Tugwell has never been known to claim practical experience as a farmer on the basis of his boyhood practice in picking apples and watching cows. Chosen to be a director of an unprecedented experiment in controlling the production of cotton, wheat, and hogs, his own preference in foods is for delicacies. He is a gourmet and accomplished in the concoction of rare salads. Dr. Tugwell attended high school in Buffalo and the Wharton School of Finance and Commerce at the University of Pennsylvania, where he remained until he had three degrees. He taught economics at Pennsylvania and Washington for brief periods before going to Columbia. He thought the orthodox textbooks on economics boring and unreal. In 1924, he and two of his colleagues, Messrs. Munro and Stryker, published a symposium entitled *American Economic Life*. For dull tables of statistics they substituted pictures of the contemporary world in its economic aspects: of a striker being beaten by police for coal and iron companies, and of Douglas Fairbanks labeled a member of "the higher income class." Two years later Dr. Tugwell published *Industry's Coming of Age*, with a prefatory indictment of the teaching of orthodox economics for continuing to "concentrate largely on the conceptual statements of a theory inherited from an old tradition."

Dr. Tugwell mingled freely with Socialists of the League of Industrial Democracy and the Civil Liberties Union. In the summer of 1927 he spent two months in Soviet Russia with a delegation of American trade unionists and intellectuals. He wrote the chapter on Russian agriculture for the symposium that came out of that expedition. The discovery that Dr. Tugwell had visited Russia was exploited to the utmost by the die-hards in Congress when they first saw the revolutionary farm bill at the special session of 1933. It happened that Dr. Tugwell's chapter on Russian agriculture had been realistic and rather critical of the agricultural policies of the Soviet régime. The audacity and determination behind the great Russian experiment stirred him. But he became neither a Socialist nor a Communist. Instead, he wrote for *The New Republic*.

Dr. Tugwell was convinced that the great American economic machine needed thorough remodeling but he was no less convinced that the plans for the new machine could not be found in imported creeds. Neither did he believe in forcible revolution. In his book *The Industrial Discipline*, he wrote: "I have never found myself greatly in sympathy with the revolutionary tactic. 'Force never settles anything' has always seemed to me a sufficient axiom. It is my reading of history that reconstruction is about as difficult after a revolutionary debacle as it would have been in a process of gradual substitution."

To Dr. Tugwell we owe the useful differentiation of a modern liberal from a radical: "Liberals would like to rebuild the station while the trains are running; radicals prefer to blow up the station and forgo service until the new structure is built."

Dr. Tugwell's winter experience in trying to get the farm bill through the lame duck Congress reinforced his conviction that he was not cut out to be a politician, and until about a week before March 4 he stubbornly refused to take the post of Assistant Secretary of Agriculture. He finally consented to go to Washington temporarily until the farm experiment had been launched. He was delighted to put on Mr. Wallace's shoulders the wearing task of handling Congressmen and farm leaders. Dr. Tugwell's activities were by no means confined to the farm experiment and preparations for the World Economic Conference. He was summoned to such varied services as explaining the banking bill to Congressmen, assisting in drafting the National Recovery Act, and preparing a plan for a stable dollar.

In nearly every situation, Dr. Tugwell is the advocate of bold and drastic action. The public works program was far too small to please him. When speculators went on their spring spree, he would have closed the stock and commodity exchanges. He demonstrated what he meant by thoroughness by having two professors draft a Pure Foods and Drugs bill which paralyzed with fright every food and drug lobbyist in Washington.

While his colleague, Professor Berle, pleads for a new order of business men inspired by higher ethics, Dr. Tugwell does not expect business men to be different from what they are until the system in which they operate is changed. When others have seen repentant industrialists and financiers eagerly co-operating in the creation of a new era, Dr. Tugwell has seen only a lot of badly scared men who will return to their old habits as soon as they dare. At the conference table, Dr. Tugwell is a tenacious fighter, but he emerges apparently unruffled. While men around him have dropped from fatigue and let their nervous systems be frazzled to the breaking point, Dr. Tugwell, cool and philosophical, has enjoyed himself hugely.

When the name of Professor Adolf Augustus Berle, Jr. first appeared on the roll of the brains trust, many people thought he was his father, whose career as a Congregational minister and scholar is traceable in

Who's Who in America. The younger Berle had not attained sufficient
fame to be listed among the thousands of learned men in that volume.
However, his remarkable intellect and his ability as a lawyer and economist were known and freely acknowledged in discriminating circles.
Before the end of 1932, his book, written with Gardiner C. Means, *The
Modern Corporation and Private Property*, established him in the front
rank of contemporary analysts and thinkers.

At 38, Mr. Berle is a former "infant prodigy" who has not ceased
to be a prodigy. He went through Harvard in three years and was
graduated with honors at seventeen. At 21 he had his LL.B. from Harvard Law School. He worked for a time in the law office of Louis D.
Brandeis. During the war his service as an army intelligence officer took
him into the Caribbean, and he added the sugar business, Latin-Ameri-
can law, and Caribbean politics and sociology to the subjects on which
he was later recognized as an expert. At 24 he went to the Peace Conference as an assistant to Frank Howard Lord, American High Commissioner to Poland, in the redrafting of the eastern frontier of Germany. He
thought the solution incorporated in the draft Treaty was indefensible.
He resigned and came home to begin the practice of law in New York
City. Through his father he had known Lillian Wald since childhood
and he began active work at the Henry Street Settlement. He also became interested in the welfare of the Indians and defended their rights
in several law suits. His main line of legal work, however, gradually carried him into accepted channels for a respectable and ambitious young
corporation lawyer in New York City. He became an active Republican. His marriage relieved him of financial cares. While continuing his
law practice he lectured at the Harvard School of Business for a time,
then joined the staff of the Columbia Law School.

Professor Berle's short and slender figure is a concentrate of nervous
and intellectual energy. Among the original membership of the brains
trust, he was the brilliant lawyer, the most thorough analytical economist, a master of prose, and a bit of a moralist. He is not lacking in
self-assurance but at times he listens with every appearance of respect-
ful attention to the long dissertations of economists, business men, and
lawyers who have not a fraction of his ability. At other times, he is an-
noyed, and he shows it. During Mr. Roosevelt's presidential campaign
he made himself an expert on federal finances, railroad rehabilitation,

banking, and control of corporations. He contributed "industrial cannon fodder" and other striking phrases and was the chief draftsman of the manifesto of the New Deal, the Commonwealth Club speech. At the short Congressional session of the winter of 1932-33, he helped to write the Bankruptcy Act.

Professor Berle could have had an important official post in the new Administration, but he preferred to be free to continue his teaching and the practice of law. Nevertheless, he spent two or three days a week in Washington during the first phase of the revolution. His presence was distressing to many of the Democratic lawyers, who, having helped to elect Mr. Roosevelt, had arrived in Washington to reap their reward in handsome legal fees as representatives of banks, corporations, and other business interests. Professor Berle seemed to have some of the clients best able to pay. The legal fraternity could not quite believe that one of their own would consider it unethical to take advantage of his standing in high places by accepting fat retainers. It developed, however, that Mr. Berle's work with the railroad executives and in helping a few large banks to reopen was as a representative of the Administration and that he received no fee.

Mr. Roosevelt made Mr. Berle special adviser to the Reconstruction Finance Corporation. There Mr. Berle tried to make sense out of prodigal loans to railroads to pay off their bankers and meet interest payments on over-capitalized corporate structures. He endeavored to use the government's position as a creditor to hasten the essential co-ordination of the railroad industry. Some of the railroad executives and financiers were flabbergasted—or pretended to be—by his suggestions. The mentality of many railroad executives is not geared to the New Deal, and re-organizations and mergers without huge profits to private bankers violate the fundamental code of Wall Street, even though they may benefit security owners.

The Agricultural Adjustment Administration sought Mr. Berle as its legal counsel during hearings on a sugar agreement. Mr. Berle's finicky sense of ethics led him to refuse on the ground that he was counsel to the American Molasses Company, which had relations with the sugar business. The NRA was already staffed with business men and labor leaders who felt no hesitation in serving because of their special interests. Excepting Mr. Berle, all the lawyers with knowledge of

sugar appeared to be employed by the big producing interests, the re-
fineries, or the Wall Street sugar banks. Mr. Berle was finally persuaded
that the AAA had no qualms about his ability to ignore the minor interests of his private client. The sugar producers and refiners found
him as exacting as the railroads had. He threw their first proposals out
the window. The refiners accused him of prejudice in favor of Cuban
refining interests. The inclusion of Cuba in an American closed sugar
area was the basic point in the Administration's program for the rehabilitation of Cuba. Early in September Mr. Roosevelt sent Mr. Berle on a
temporary mission to Cuba as financial adviser to the U.S. Embassy. He
arrived just as the second revolution broke out, spent a few futile days
there, and returned to Washington.

During the hundred-day session of Congress, Mr. Berle had a hand
in such varied pieces of legislation as the Banking Act, the new Securities Act, and the National Recovery Act. When the banks were on the
operating table during the moratorium, he would have done a thorough
job of surgery. He was overruled. The Glass-Steagall Banking Act and
the Securities Act were both disappointments to him, and he at once
went to work to draft amendments or substitute bills to be presented to
the 1934 session of Congress. In the summer of 1933, he helped to sift
the various schemes for a commodity dollar. Mr. Berle clings doggedly
to his hope that bankers and business men and lawyers will realize that
restraint, higher standards of conduct, and a social point of view are imperative if the capitalistic régime is to survive, even in a modified form.
In speeches to bankers he reminds them that in England it is supposed
to be a high social offense for a banker to make a large personal fortune.

When Mr. Berle inserts his mind in a problem he pushes through
until he has located the last isolated detail and put it in its proper place.
He is able to draw back and get a bird's-eye view. His book with Mr.
Means, *The Modern Corporation and Private Property*, is based on the
most elaborate studies that have been made of the growth of American
corporations, but the masses of detail rise steadily to well-formed conclusions. In summing up, Messrs. Berle and Means wrote: "The rise of
the modern corporation has brought a concentration of economic power
which can compete on equal terms with the modern state—economic
power versus political power, each strong in its own field. The state seeks
in some aspects to regulate the corporation, while the corporation, stead-

ily becoming more powerful, makes every effort to avoid such regulation. Where its own interests are concerned, it even attempts to dominate the state. The future may see the economic organism, now typified by the corporation, not only on an equal plane with the state, but possibly even superseding it as the dominant form of social organization. The law of corporations, accordingly, might well be considered as a potential constitutional law for the new economic state, while business practice is increasingly assuming the aspects of economic statesmanship."

These men—Moley, Tugwell, and Berle—are inseparable from the Roosevelt Revolution. No list of the six or eight most important architects and builders of the new régime would be valid without them. Next to Mr. Roosevelt, Mr. Moley was the most important, in or out of the Cabinet. With Messrs. Tugwell and Berle would have to be ranked Mr. Douglas, chiefly because of his restraining influence on certain occasions during the first months; Louis Howe, in devious and indefinable ways; Frances Perkins, Hugh S. Johnson, Harold L. Ickes, and probably Henry A. Wallace and George N. Peek. A line arbitrarily drawn there excludes many like James A. Farley, who were important in the political management, and others who, though farther removed from the center of action, clearly understood the significance of the experiment.

Specialists and social scientists of liberal thought are still being drawn into the government. Subsidiary brains trusts have sprung up around every important experiment of the New Deal.

In the agricultural brains trust one finds: M. L. Wilson, who helped show the world how to produce wheat on a large scale and then had to invent a plan for reducing the wheat output; Mordecai Ezekiel, the brilliant young economist and part author of the revolutionary farm bill, who can demonstrate by logarithms how to raise hogs; William I. Myers, former Professor of Farm Finance at Cornell, the chief author of the Farm Mortgage Act, now Deputy Governor of the Farm Credit Administration; Herman Oliphant, former Professor of Law at Johns Hopkins; Gardiner C. Means, Mr. Berle's associate at Columbia; Louis Bean and the staff of the Bureau of Agricultural Economics; Howard E. Babcock, former Professor of Marketing at Cornell; Dr. Frederic H. Howe.

In the monetary brains trust may be found: O. M. W. Sprague, former Professor of Banking and Finance at Harvard, whom Mr. Roosevelt took away from the Bank of England and installed as Special Assistant to the Secretary of the Treasury; Professor Warren of Cornell, one of the leading authorities on the commodity dollar; James H. Rogers, Professor of Political Economy at Yale, another currency specialist.

The National Recovery Administration brought together such men as: Alexander Sachs, who made a reputation by his accuracy in forecasting the course of the depression and then began charting the recovery; Leo Wolman, a member of the faculty of the New School for Social Research, and authority on labor problems; Earle Dean Howard, Professor of Economics at Northwestern.

Among the former academic men scattered here and there are: John Dickinson, former Professor of Law at the University of Pennsylvania, in the post of Assistant Secretary of Commerce; Isador Lubin, former Professor of Economics at the University of Missouri, installed as chief of the statistical division of the Department of Labor; W. M. W. Splawn, former Professor of Economics at the University of Texas, as adviser to the House Committee on Interstate Commerce and one of the leading assistants to Joseph B. Eastman in handling the railroad problem; Arthur E. Morgan, former President of Antioch College, as Chairman of the Board of the Tennessee Valley Authority; Harcourt A. Morgan, former Dean of the School of Agriculture of the University of Tennessee, as another member of the board of the Tennessee Valley Authority.

One could name twenty or more liberal lawyers in the Administration: Donald Richberg, Counsel to the NRA; Jerome Frank, Counsel to AAA; and many of Felix Frankfurter's protégés. Mr. Frankfurter refused to accept the post of Solicitor General but he responded heartily to the invitation to suggest men to fill many of the legal posts. Mr. Roosevelt appointed a dozen or more men wholly or chiefly on Mr. Frankfurter's recommendation. Of these the most prominent are Dean G. Acheson, Under-Secretary of the Treasury, and David E. Lilienthal, the third member of the Tennessee Valley Authority, and Professor James Landis, former Professor at Harvard Law School, member of the Federal Trade Commission.

The men of the diffused brains trust represent many shades of thought and many specialties. In most of them two characteristics stand out: enthusiasm for the American experiment and unabating criticism of the course of its development. None of the easy optimism or pessimism of men accustomed to gauging the world by the stock market or the momentary profits or losses of their business is to be found in this group. Free competition in ideas and frank criticism are basic characteristics of the Roosevelt Administration. Probably never before in its history has the Federal Government found important roles for so many men of fertile and courageous minds.

part two

THE
IMPERIAL
JESSE JONES

One of the realities the President had to deal with was the fact that some administrators in his official family were "stars" in their own right. Such a luminary was Jesse Jones, at first Chairman of the Board of the Reconstruction Finance Corporation, and later Secretary of Commerce. The brief article reprinted here is interesting not only because it tells us something about Jones, but also because of the clear voice it gives to the attitude of American business toward the New Deal in 1940 as interpreted by *Fortune Magazine*. Hence, we hear from what was probably the most serious mass publication on business in the United States the familiar criticism of the Administration—that precious few bureaucrats had ever met a payroll.

Jesse Jones

Fortune Magazine

Jesse Holman Jones is probably the only man in a position of great influence in the Roosevelt Administration who knows in his guts what it feels like for a businessman to lay a million dollars on the line. Not that that is the sine qua non of an administrator in a democratic government, but that is the quality that sets Jesse Jones apart from the rest of those around Franklin Roosevelt. It is one reason why Jesse is in Washington at all—and also why he is not in high favor with New Dealers. Mr. Roosevelt was born a *rentier*, and many times has reiterated his belief in the profit system; Henry Morgenthau is a rich man's son who would be considerably disturbed at losing his wealth; and there are plenty of others in the Administration who subscribe in theory to the processes of capitalism. But with the possible execption of Marriner Eccles—a banker who operates in an intellectual cosmos of his own—Jesse Jones is probably the only man in the New Deal who fully understands and appreciates that subtle nuance that makes a businessman decide whether to go to the market place for money to build a plant or get along as best he may by cleverly using depreciation reserves.

For proof of this one need go no further than the preceding account of his stewardship of the Reconstruction Finance Corporation. Certainly no other agency in Washington holds out such glittering dreams of power to the reformer as does RFC. It might be trying to run the railroads; it might be trying to run the banks; it might be trying to energize

"Jesse Jones," *Fortune Magazine*, XXI (May, 1940), 140-44. *Reprinted by permission.*

the business process instead of simply offering it credit. Not that RFC doesn't have a voice in these things, some factor of power; it does and should. But it is not trying to *run* them. RFC has been a tantalizing compromise between the forces of further government intervention in business and those who would follow a laissez faire policy. And it is this that has made RFC something of an enigma of state capitalism. It is no enigma, however, when you come to know Jesse Jones.

Jesse, of course, does not conceive of himself as an arbitrator. He does not delude himself that he is leading the U.S. into the beatitude of a Swedish middle way. He has no such highfalutin notions and he is no intellectual: the very thought of being one would cause distinct tremors in his viscera. Jesse is a man who *feels;* and his feeling carries him along a line that is different from that of Mr. Hoover, who hesitated to propose RFC, and the New Dealers, who believe it should go on to bigger things. Jesse feels that RFC is great precisely because it is needed by capitalism and yet has not jimmied the system.

The qualities that make Jesse Jones the despair not only of New Dealers but of rugged individualists are readily understandable. For all his success, Jesse never achieved the position, say, of Walter Chrysler or Alfred Sloan, whose devotion to a single business is their life. Jesse Jones could have been a lumber baron (he once owned sixty-five yards and three sawmills); he could have been a banker (he is Chairman of the National Bank of Commerce, Houston's second-biggest bank); he could have been a newspaper publisher (he owns the Houston *Chronicle* and holds the purse strings on the Houston *Post*); he could have been a hotel man or a real-estate operator (he owns some forty buildings in Houston, including the tallest skyscraper and the Rice Hotel, not to mention half the office space in Fort Worth); he could have been a radio magnate (he admits owning two of Houston's three stations and hedges on whether he owns the third). But the fact is that Jesse Jones was a promoter *who built a city, not a business.*

You can't build a city, of course, without making enemies—and Jesse has plenty of enemies in Houston. You can't be a promoter and a trader (a shrewd trader, his friends say, a hard and ruthless one, say his enemies) without becoming labeled "Ten Per Cent Jones" by those who don't like you. But whether friend or enemy, everyone in Jesse Jones's home town is in complete agreement on one thing: he built

Houston up from a one-night stand on Buffalo Bayou into the second-largest and fastest-growing metropolis in the South. Jesse Jones played business as Charlie Schwab played roulette—all over the board.

That accomplishment, however, is not one that will wed a man to the business process. But it does give a man a wider feeling of power, and the sure knowledge that the mechanisms of government can be used in the active service of the profit motive. It frees a man from the distrust of government that so often obsessed those wedded to a single business. It gives to Jesse the broader, less circumspect point of view that allows him to flirt with the Circes of the New Deal without ever being caught *flagrante delicto*.

The actual story of how Jesse Jones came into his position of power in the New Deal is interesting in its relationship to the national economy. Jesse, in Washington, is a representative of southern Democracy. And southern Democracy is *sui generis*. It possesses a distrust of Wall Street business but has an absolute devotion to southern business. Broadly, its position with respect to the New Deal has been that it has gone along on economic reforms, those tending to lessen Wall Street's control of the business process, but has quarreled with the Administration on social reforms, e.g., the Wagner Act and Wages and Hours. And southern Democracy, while it does not control as it did from the days of Calhoun to Jefferson Davis, does have a balance of power on Capitol Hill. Thus when the Hoover Administration finally revived the War Finance Corporation in the form of RFC, it was beholden to three southern Democrats for getting the act passed—Joe Robinson, the Democratic leader in the Senate; Carter Glass; and Jack Garner, Speaker of the House. These men naturally had to be consulted in selecting RFC's Board. Robinson picked his close friend Harvey Couch, which was satisfactory to Mr. Hoover; but Hoover, who disliked Garner thoroughly, didn't want him to have the power of naming a Director but only of making a choice. So from Glass and other Southerners, Mr. Hoover obtained a list of five men and asked Garner to take his pick. Jesse Jones's name was last on the list and Garner said: "Mr. President, that's a kangaroo list." "What do you mean?" Mr. Hoover asked. "Why all its strength is in its hindquarters." Jesse got the appointment.

That was in 1932 and Jesse was then but forty-eight years old. Born in the Cumberland River country of Tennessee, the son of a prosperous farmer, Jesse had been in Texas since he was twenty. He had quickly reached beyond the lumberyard of his uncle in Dallas, where he had got his start. He had spread to Houston and had established himself in the lumber business over much of Texas, Oklahoma, and New Mexico. He had come through the panic of 1907 as Jesse Jones the Builder. He had become big—and that was but the beginning of it. By 1917 he had become big enough to be a dollar-a-year man in Washington with the Red Cross. By 1924 he had become finance director of the Democratic campaign; and by 1928 he had become enough of a power to get the Democratic National Convention for Houston. He had arrived on the national scene. If he wasn't the biggest man in Texas, he was big enough to make it worth arguing about. And he was wedded to no business. Thus when Washington beckoned, Jesse was quick to respond.

That Jesse has loved Washington, that he has cherished the power that has accumulated in his hands, is obvious. He has held on through some tough years. Trying to scalp Jesse has been a favorite sport with New Dealers. They delighted in taking away RFC's authority over self-liquidating projects, for example, and giving it to Harold Ickes's less stringent PWA. But it is the measure of Jesse Jones as a Texas bull-dogger, just as it is the measure of the timelessness of the power of southern Democracy, that it is Jesse Jones and not Ickes who is handling the federal financing of the newest big self-liquidating project—the tunnel under the East River from Manhattan to Brooklyn. Certainly, in his seven years under the New Deal, Jesse has made compromises. But to call Jesse a Uriah Heep is to miss the essence. He is not two-faced about it. He does not pretend to like the New Deal and inwardly hate it. Jesse is concerned primarily with RFC and its affiliates—and he likes them fine. They have become part of him—and he of them. He wouldn't like them if they had become something else—but it has been his job to see that they didn't.

It has been a hard job, too. For Jesse works hard. He gets up at six-thirty and starts reading office papers before breakfast. But he doesn't work until one or two in the morning any more, as he did in RFC's early days. Not that his health isn't good, for it is—and Jesse is wise enough to conserve it. And for relaxation there is always the telephone. He probably spends half his day on the telephone—much of it long distance.

Jesse's friends are always saying he is the biggest individual contributor to A.T.&T.'s $9 dividend.

Jesse Jones, of course, couldn't have been around the New Deal so long without absorbing some of its spiritual qualities. Away from the immediate ornery task of bossing his investments in Houston, Jesse has softened in his attitude toward government and its responsibility to society. He believes in keeping the Big Stick of government handy to use on the big boys if they oppress the little fellow; he believes in slum clearance and the like; he believes it is proper to use the instrumentality of government to help the underprivileged third. But he has none of the New Deal's faith in the perfectibility of the underprivileged; he has little faith that they will ever rise above themselves; he feels that they are apt to take their slums with them. His liberalism is the paternal liberalism of a man of wealth that is fed by the irresistibly paternalistic influence of big government.

And just as Jesse has loved Washington, so has Washington loved him. It has never tired of pointing him out to visitors: his handsome appearance, his six-foot-three of height, his white hair and black brows, his mildness and strangely dimpled cheeks. Washington has seen too many of the loud, backslapping Texans like Amon Carter not to appreciate Jesse Jones. And Washington, always loving a fight, has enjoyed Jesse's tiffs with the New Dealers and has admired the way that Jesse's warm blue eyes, withal have retained their soft laughter. Washington knows that Jesse could never have gone back to Houston without getting bedsore of inaction; and it has applauded him for holding on. And when the Washington *cognoscenti* banter Jesse about riding close herd on RFC, they know Jesse couldn't face his cronies around Buffalo Bayou again if he didn't turn a better deal for the government than Gene Meyer, the Wall Street boy, had turned. Then, too, Washington is somewhat grateful to Jesse Jones. It was skeptical of this Texas trader when he first came in 1932; it was suspicious of him. As Turner Catledge once noted: the town always expected Jesse Jones to take the Washington Monument down to Houston. And Washington has felt grateful to Jesse simply because he didn't.

part three

THE
PERSONAL
DIMENSION
OF BUREAUCRACY

The following pages, taken from Interior Secretary Harold L. Ickes's *Secret Diaries,* tell us much about the President's relationships with his subordinates, particularly the difficult ones. We see Ickes's concern about and even jealousy of Hopkins, his antipathy to Morgenthau, his impatience with Miss Perkins, his distrust of McIntyre, and his disillusionment with the President himself. We also get some hints about the bureaucrat's contacts with Congress, with the press, and with party politics. Finally, we see the Roosevelt "treatment" being applied to the unhappy bureaucrat. It is interesting to note that nearly all Ickes really got out of the luncheon meeting was tea and sympathy.

The Administrator's Viewpoint

Harold L. Ickes

Wednesday, May 13, 1936

After thinking the matter over carefully, I have come to the conclusion that I cannot talk to Hopkins as I suggested to the President I would do at our conference on Saturday. I know full well that he would not yield any of the authority granted him under the pending bill and I do not propose to put myself in the position of a suppliant to him. I shall tell the President the next time I see him—and I have asked for an appointment—that there is no use of my talking to Hopkins and that only he can settle the issues involved.

Until I came back from my talk with the President on Saturday I really did not realize the extraordinary powers granted to Hopkins under this bill. The huge sum of almost $1.5 billion is granted outright to the Works Progress Administrator, which means Hopkins. The only power originally reserved to the President was the right to determine wage scales and that was the hot end of the program. Even that has been cut out by an amendment. While the bill purports to break down the appropriation into several classes of permissible expenditures, in effect it gives Hopkins blanket authority to spend this huge sum of money as, when, and where he pleases, without check or hindrance from anyone, not even from the President himself. Having granted the money, Congress will have no control nor will the courts have any power to

Harold L. Ickes, *The Secret Diary of Harold L. Ickes*, Volume I, *The First Thousand Days* (New York: Simon and Schuster, Inc., 1953), pp. 585-97. *Reprinted by permission of the publishers.*

interfere. Of course, Hopkins could be removed by the President for cause and he could be impeached by the Congress. To all effects and purposes, however, here is a man who is given the largest sum of money in the history of this country, except to the President himself under previous bills, to administer in his uncontrolled discretion. I doubt whether in all history any comparable man has been given such power. It is an extraordinary situation.

Last session Hopkins was afraid to appear before the Appropriations Committee of the Senate and hid out in Florida. I saved the bill for the President in the form in which he wanted it. In order to get the bill through Congress the President had to have the appropriation run to himself and give the assurance that he would be the Administrator. At that time Hopkins was poison to both branches of Congress. While I had a good many enemies up there, the tide was beginning to run heavily in my favor. I think Congress would not have objected to me as Administrator, but it would not have listened to the suggestion of Hopkins as Administrator. Even now the overwhelming sentiment, both in the House and the Senate, is against Hopkins and his program, notwithstanding which the House has voted him this extraordinary sum of money without any restraint worth mentioning. Under the bill as it stands and as explained by Chairman Buchanan of the Appropriations Committee, neither the President nor Hopkins could grant money to PWA, to Resettlement, or to any other Federal agency even if he wanted to. All the money had to be expended under the personal direction of WPA.

Senator Guffey came in to see me Thursday morning at his own instance. He announced that he had nothing to ask of me but merely wanted to say that he thought I had been given pretty rough treatment in connection with this relief bill. He said that Hopkins was clearly a candidate for President in 1940 and he referred to his close connection with Frank Hague, of Jersey City, and Mayor Kelly, of Chicago. He asked me where Hopkins got his influence with the President and I told him that I had been told that it was through Mrs. Roosevelt and the President's mother. It was in connection with this statement that he made the comment he did about Hague and Kelly.

He criticized Hopkins' program and Hopkins' administration of that program. On the contrary, he said I had done a fine job and an honest job. He went on to say that his leaders in Pennsylvania thought that I was the man for President in 1940. I told him this was flattering but that I was not a candidate for anything. His reply was a repetition of what he had already said and he added that his people were for me, not because I was a Pennsylvanian, but because I had done a fine and honest job as PWA Administrator and for the further reason that I was the only man in the Administration who could stand up on the platform and make a forthright speech on the issues. He added that I was the only member of the Cabinet who could make a decent speech. As he left he told me to call on him for any service that he could perform. This interview not only surprised me, it touched me. I had never met Guffey until I came to Washington and certainly I have never regarded him as much of an idealist. He is close to Farley and a loyal supporter of the President. That he should have made the statement to me that he did was highly gratifying and, of course, his references to 1940 were more than complimentary.

Tom Corcoran also came in to see me on Tuesday. The reason for his call was to find out whether I would have any objection to Foley's being urged for appointment as a United States judge in New York. I told him that I was committed to Margold, but neither he nor I think that Margold has a chance of being appointed. I assured him that I would not stand in the way of any man on my staff advancing himself. Jocularly I asked Corcoran whether he couldn't find a nice, soft berth for me. Then, to my surprise, he said that there was one place in the Administration that he thought I was pretty well fitted for, although he imagined that it would not particularly appeal to me. He referred to the Comptroller Generalship. McCarl's term expires next month. This is a fifteen-year appointment at $10,000 a year.

I asked Corcoran whether he was responsible for the story that appeared in a Washington paper the other day to the effect that Senator Harrison and I were the leading candidates for this place. I told him that it had given me a good laugh, and that the Comptrollership had never occurred to me and did not appeal to me. He said that I was in the unfortunate position of being the only real conservationist in the Administration and at the same time the best qualified man for this office. He added that I am that rare combination, an honest administrator, adding that there were many honest men but few good administrators. He pointed out that the Comptroller Generalship was the most powerful office in the Government barring only the Presidency, and with this view I agreed, as I have had ample opportunity to learn from personal experience with McCarl just how powerful this office is. I ventured the guess that Henry Morgenthau would be able to secure the selection of one of his hand-picked men for this place.

He told me of a talk with Felix Frankfurter during which Frankfurter had said that, after canvassing the situation pretty generally in the country, he had come to the conclusion that only two men in the Administration had enhanced their reputations during their connection with it. The two men he mentioned were Secretary Hull and myself. Corcoran and I touched very lightly on the Hopkins situation. I told him that if I had wanted to make trouble, I could have stirred up a lot of it but that I had kept hands off. Corcoran said that that was the difference between a fair fighter and a man who would use any implement to fight with.

Meanwhile lines of battle are forming in the Senate. Senator Hayden yesterday introduced an amendment to the bill providing for a separate appropriation of $700 million for PWA. I don't expect for a minute that he will be able to pass this amendment, but the bill itself represents sound tactics at this stage. Senator Vandenberg offered a substitute bill. I understand that Senator Norris went to the President on Monday and strongly supported PWA as against WPA. Word came to me this morning that not only Norris but Johnson and La Follette had sent word to Hayden that they would support him in his efforts to get money for PWA. In the meanwhile, members of the PWA staff are hard at work preparing a statement of what we have done and are capable of doing in anticipation of my being called before the Senate Appropriations Committee, as it appears that I will be either on Friday or Monday. I understand that other outside pressure is being brought to bear on the President. It is being pointed out to him that he is not only making a grave mistake from the point of view of relief administration but one equally as grave from the political point of view. It seems quite clear to me that if this bill goes through substantially as it is and no further appropriation is made for PWA, I shall have no other course than to resign.

Saturday, May 16, 1936

The last two days have been eventful and busy ones. I started in on Wednesday afternoon to try to get an appointment with the President without success. I wanted to follow up my interview of last Saturday with the President, but McIntyre seems to be playing Hopkins' game now and I haven't been able to get through him. Of course, I could get through Miss Le Hand but I hate to do that, except in extreme cases. I had been asked to appear before the subcommittee of the Appropriations Committee of the Senate to give a review of the work of PWA, and members of my staff have been working desperately to get a statement in shape for me. First, I was scheduled to appear Thursday afternoon but as this conflicted with the regular Cabinet meeting, I called up Senator Adams and told him I would come Friday morning at ten o'clock.

At Cabinet meeting Thursday afternoon, after the President had gone the usual rounds, he began to talk about the work-relief program. There was no doubt that he was addressing his remarks to me. I don't know who had told him that I was expecting to go before the subcommittee as a witness, although I had intended to do that at the conclusion of the Cabinet meeting. That he knew, there was no doubt, for he told me that he didn't want me to give any figures that he had not seen in advance. In this connection he told me that the figures I had submitted to him last Saturday were all wrong, but how he could say that I cannot understand because I believed then, and I believe now, that they were accurate. Probably Hopkins and his minions had been given a chance to knock them down.

I told the President that perhaps it would be better for me not to go before the committee at all, since I did not care to make a statement that was not full and free and frank. Then he talked about indirect employment, taking the line that he usually takes in that regard. He didn't want me to give any figures on indirect employment, and my reply was that since one of the objects of the PWA program was to stimulate indirect employment, no picture of PWA would be accurate without figures on indirect employment. We hammered back and forth at each other on this subject and it was plain to see that the President was not in the best of temper. Neither was I, if the truth be told, although I kept good control of myself without, however, weakening at any point.

The President said that I must not criticize the program of WPA and that it would be a criticism of that program if I should show to the subcommittee what PWA had done. He added that if the Congress should earmark for PWA any of the money proposed to be appropriated for the Works Progress Administration, he would veto the bill.

I was pretty angry by this time. It was as clear as day that the President was spanking me hard before the full Cabinet and I resented that too. All the other members appeared to be embarrassed, but I could see Henry Morgenthau stealing a covert glance at me from time to time. Doubtless he enjoyed the spanking very much.

When the President had gone down the line of the Cabinet, I had told him that I wanted to speak to him for a minute after the Cabinet meeting. As a matter of fact, what I had in mind was to say that I had been called before the Adams subcommittee. However, before I could get to the President at the conclusion of the meeting, George Dern had crowded in ahead of me to show the President some figures in a book dealing with the Florida canal project. Then Miss Perkins, as usual, shifted in ahead on the other side and began to chatter about some legislation, although the President had said that he could not be delayed because he was going out on the south lawn to meet a delegation of Navajo and Pueblo Indians. I caught Miss Perkins' eye and indicated that I wished she would withdraw, but although she understood what I was driving at, she went on. Then I stalked out of the Cabinet room in no very good temper. I wanted an opportunity then and there to tell the President that he had put me in an untenable position, having in mind to follow promptly with my written resignation.

After I got back to my office, Miss Perkins called me up to explain that she had purposely not responded to my signal to betake herself off because she knew the President so very well and knew that it was a mistake when he was in that sort of humor to allow things to crystallize, this being her precise expression. She begged me not to let things crystallize until he had had two or three days to come to himself. She said that plainly he was under some great personal pressure. I told her that so far as I was concerned, matters had crystallized and that even the President couldn't spank me publicly.

Before Miss Perkins called me, I had already called for one of my personal secretaries, as well as for Slattery and Burlew. Then I proceeded to dictate a resignation both as Secretary of the Interior and as Public

Works Administrator. I didn't call Mike Straus in on this because my mind was made up and I knew that he would hang around my neck like a heavy weight trying to dissuade me from a course of action that I was determined upon. Wishing an outside newspaperman's point of view, I called up James Waldo Fawcett at the *Evening Star* office and asked him to come over. We worked on the letter until almost seven o'clock, when I suggested that we go home for dinner and return afterward. At that time it was then in the minds of all of us that my resignation ought to go to the White House Thursday night.

In the meantime, Tom Corcoran came in to see me. I told him what had happened at Cabinet meeting, but I did not tell him that I was working on my resignation because I knew, first, that he would attempt to dissuade me and, second, that he might let the matter drop at the White House in advance of my resignation reaching the President's hand. I did indicate to him, however, that I had come pretty nearly to the end of my rope and he said he hoped that I wouldn't do anything for at least a day or two. He, too, told me, with some specifications, that the President had been under great personal pressure. He said that he was having trouble with Morgenthau because Morgenthau had made such an ass of himself in connection with the pending revenue bill. Corcoran deprecated what the President has been doing with respect to PWA and he also thinks it is a great mistake to give $1.5 billion to Hopkins to spend in his uncontrolled discretion. He wanted to go to Hiram Johnson and talk the matter over with him to see if he would espouse the cause of PWA. I told him that whatever he wanted to do would be all right with me, but that, personally, I was not particularly interested in the matter.

Thursday night Burlew, Slattery, Fawcett, and I again met in my office and we whipped into shape a rather long letter in which I presented my resignation and gave reasons supporting my action. My original idea had been to write a very short resignation, covering less than a page of letter paper. However, my three advisers thought I ought to give my reasons, in fact, prepare a document which would state my case to the public. We also decided, however, that there was no imperative necessity of sending the resignation to the White House that night. When we finally left my office after eleven o'clock, the resignation along the line that we were working was practically in final shape.

I got to the office early Friday morning and made certain corrections in the letter. These corrections were merely matters of form and not of substance. But all the way to my office and while I was working over this first draft for the last time, I could not rid myself of the notion that it would be a mistake to send that particular letter to the President. It was simply a knockout and left him no recourse. It was a fighting letter and while I was prepared to fight and was really looking forward to a separation from a service which has been so distasteful to me in many particulars, I did not think it was quite fair to kick the President in the face before closing the door. So I called my three advisers together again and after discussing the matter they agreed with me, whereupon I dictated a further draft as follows:

The Secretary of the Interior
Washington, May 14, 1936

My dear Mr. President:

I find myself differing fundamentally with your work-relief program as extended and modified under the bill now pending before the Senate. As I see it, the passage of this bill as written will destroy the Public Works Administration, a purpose which was indicated in statements made by you at recent press conferences by which, in effect, you repudiated PWA and indicated a lack of confidence in me as Administrator. Little doubt of your attitude in this matter remains in my mind in view of your statement at the Cabinet meeting today when your orders made it impossible for me to respond to the request of the Senate Appropriations Committee to present a statement of what PWA has accomplished to date.

In the circumstances, I have no option except to tender my resignation, both as Secretary of the Interior and as Administrator of Public Works. This I hereby do with my thanks to you for the opportunity that you have given me to serve the country and with profound regret that the situation makes this action necessary. I hope that you will accept this resignation, to take effect at your earliest convenience.

Sincerely yours,
(Signed) Harold L. Ickes
Secretary of the Interior

The President
The White House

Wishing to get this letter into the President's hands without going through McIntyre, I called Miss Le Hand to tell her I was sending her a letter to the President. She said she would give it to him. I sent it over between ten and eleven o'clock. In the meantime, McIntyre had called me to ask me whether I could lunch with the President at one. This was the appointment that I had been trying to get for the previous couple of days, but I think it also meant that the President was feeling a little sorry for his actions at Cabinet meeting. While I was working on my resignation, Tom Corcoran came in to see me again. I think he was worried as to what I might do. He brought Ben Cohen with him and they both urged me to stick it out at least for a few months longer. I reminded them that they have been coming to me periodically begging me to "stick it out" for a few months longer but that matters had reached the point where I couldn't stand it much longer. All this without telling them that I was actually on the point of sending in my resignation. They both admitted that I had had a rough deal and they deprecated the action of the President both at Cabinet meeting and in his support of the Hopkins program. Corcoran wanted to know whether I had any objection to his going to the White House to suggest that there might be a way out all around, with a general saving of face, if the bill could be amended so as to give certain enlarged powers to RFC under which a considerable PWA program could be financed. I told Tom he could do as he pleased, but I did not want the President to think that he was representing me or that I had sent him.

Naturally, I didn't want McIntyre to know what was doing, so I told him I would lunch with the President at one. After Miss Le Hand had had a chance to give my letter to the President, I called her, told of my engagement with the President for luncheon, and said that perhaps in the circumstances the President would not want me to come. She said that she was sure he did because she had just come from his office and that he had told her I was lunching with him. I asked her whether he had read my letter and she said he had. I asked her nevertheless to find out discreetly whether he really wanted me. She called me back shortly and told me the President was expecting me.

When I went into his office shortly after one o'clock, Jesse Jones was about to leave. As Jesse left, the President looked at me with an expression of mock reproach and then, without saying a word, he handed me a memorandum in his own handwriting as follows:

The White House
Washington

Dear Harold—

1. P.W.A. is not "repudiated."
2. P.W.A. is not "ended."
3. I did not "make it impossible for you to go before the committee."
4. I have not indicated lack of confidence.
5. I have *full* confidence in you.
6. You and I have the same big objectives.
7. You are needed, to carry on a big common task.
8. Resignation *not* accepted!

Your affectionate friend,
(signed) Franklin D. Roosevelt

I read this communication and was quite touched by its undoubted generosity and its evident sincerity of tone. I had gone expecting that he might say that he did not want me to resign, although my resignation was in no sense a bluff. I also had in mind, if he wanted me to continue with his Administration, to discuss with him quite frankly certain matters that I have objected to. This I proceeded to do. I told him that on various occasions I had learned from the newspapers of the issuance of important Executive Orders vitally affecting matters within my jurisdiction. He asked me to give him an example and offhand I gave him three. One example was the Executive Order issued last summer which in effect wiped out PWA. At that time, after talking the matter over with Hiram Johnson, I called the President by telephone to ask for an immediate appointment that evening. Failing to get that, I told him very frankly over the telephone what I thought about the matter and he issued a modifying and explanatory statement in which, in effect, the Executive Order was recalled, but there never was any doubt what the intention was.

Another example that I gave him was the Executive Order making Dr. Gruening Reconstruction Administrator for Puerto Rico without consulting me. The President said he thought I had recommended Gruening, but I told him that I had written him a letter telling him that I would make a suggestion if he desired one but that no request for a suggestion had ever come. I told him that the Department of the Interior should have been made the agency in this case, in which event Gruening would have been the person to run the show. I pointed out to him that there was no check on Gruening unless the President was checking on him, a suggestion that he promptly negatived, and that there might be a first-class blowout one of these days in Puerto Rico for which he and I would be held responsible, when I had no authority in the matter. He suggested an amendment to this order which would give me immediate supervisory authority. The third instance I cited was with reference to the youth movement.

I recalled to the President that at no time had I been consulted with respect to the continuance of the relief program and that no information had been given to me except through the newspapers. Then I brought up the question of housing and there were one or two other matters that I frankly took up with him.

I must say that the President took everything in the best possible spirit. He told me that he was not going to discontinue PWA and that there were two or three plans that he had in mind for working matters out. It seems that someone had already said to him that instead of the $1.5 billion going to Hopkins as WPA Administrator it should go to the President. I urged him very strongly to have the bill amended in the Senate in this respect. I pointed out that WPA could be the biggest joint in our armor during the coming campaign. I said that, whether justly or unjustly, Hopkins was being criticized in all parts of the country, and that while I had no opinion to express as to the justice of any of these criticisms, I did think that it was not a good time for him to be thumbing his nose at the country as he would be doing if he allowed a bill to go through that would give Hopkins greater power and authority than had ever been given to anyone in history.

The President said that Hopkins, of course, would take any suggestions from him. I told him that undoubtedly he would but that under the bill he wouldn't have to. In that event the only recourse of the President would be to discharge him, and I said that a good deal of damage might be done before the President would be able to get around to that even if he wanted to. Even then, if Hopkins should be let out as Administrator, his successor would have the same powers.

The President has in mind that through widening the powers of RFC and by some contributions from the WPA fund to us as grants, it would be possible to go ahead with a considerable PWA program. As a matter of fact, I know this can be done because we have been working on an amendment to the law here which, however, I have not disclosed to the President, although at this session with him I told him that we had an amendment which I would like to send him for his consideration. He said that he would call in Jones and Hopkins and me and work out a plan of action. At this point I jocularly remarked that a simple person like me would be at a disadvantage sitting down with three candidates for the Presidency. The President had a good laugh at this and remarked, "Well, two anyhow," meaning, I think, Jones and himself. I did not follow up the matter, although more and more people are coming to believe that Hopkins is an active candidate.

Wednesday afternoon my bill changing the name of this Department to that of Conservation passed the Senate, thanks to the clever generalship of Senator Robinson. I at once called the President and asked him if he would let me get a rule in the House. I told him if we got the rule we would pass the bill through the House easily. He said he would. During our talk on Friday he told me that he had sent word to Speaker Byrns that he wanted a rule on this bill and that he believed we had a good chance of getting the legislation through.

This led him to discuss the reorganization of the executive branch of the Government, which I think he really has very much at heart. Among other things he is developing in his own mind a theory of having two or three executive assistants each of whom would coordinate certain departments, take care of routine matters, and bring to him others for consideration. I told him I thought this would be a good plan, as it would save him a lot of time and trouble. As a matter of fact, as I have said on other occasions, I marvel at his ability to handle the mass of detail that he finds in his lap from day to day.

As an example of the matters that were brought to him, the President made a statement which came nearer to being a criticism of Morgenthau than any I have ever heard. He said that Henry had to get in to see him at least four times a week to tell him what francs were selling at or how he believed the next bond issue would go, and that on the other days of the week he had to call him by telephone to give him the same information. He said that with an executive assistant it wouldn't be necessary for him to have to take care of such small details. I made no comment.

Among other things that I have been objecting to, as I said to the President, was the disposition on the part of several men on my staff to short-cut me to the White House. I mentioned this to the President.

Along toward the end of our interview the President said: "My dear fellow, you mustn't get any idea that I am working at cross-purposes with you," to which I replied: "Mr. President, I have a real affection for you and I hope you know that at all times I have been loyal. It will always be my purpose to work out things as you want them worked out, but I would like to know what is going on with respect to matters under me before they get too far along."

part four

ROOSEVELT
LECTURES
HIS
BUREAUCRATS

The following extract reprinted from the December 11, 1934, meeting of the National Emergency Council transcript gives the reader of history that most intriguing of opportunities—to be a mouse in the corner, an unseen witness to the deliberations among the highest public figures. Unfortunately there are no transcripts or systematic reports of cabinet meetings during the New Deal. However, the verbatim records of Roosevelt's National Emergency Council are preserved for posterity. The few pages of these *Proceedings* printed below demonstrate clearly some of the minor as well as some of the major administrative problems which arose. They demonstrate even better the capacity of FDR for assuming the role of schoolmaster and even disciplinarian in his formal contacts with his aides.

Proceedings

National Emergency Council

Mr. Richberg [Executive Director, National Emergency Council]:

There are three suggestions I would like to bring forward; the first is that there should be a definite understanding as to the manner in which departments and agencies seeking legislation will clear their proposal prior to submission to any member of Congress.

President Roosevelt:

This is tremendously important. Before any department goes up to Congress, we have got to know what they are going to ask of the sub-committees. Last year I was quite horrified—not once, but half a dozen times—by reading in the paper that some department or agency was after this, that, or the other without my knowledge.

Secretary Roper [Commerce]:

We channeled through the Director of the Budget.

President Roosevelt:

That was for appropriations. That is a different thing. What I am talking about is legislation. In matters relating to appropriations, you cannot go under the wall through a committee of Congress and ask for something different from what has been referred by the Director of the

The transcripts of the *Proceedings of the National Emergency Council* are maintained in the National Archives in Washington, D.C. They are also printed in Lester G. Seligman and Elmer E. Cornwell, Jr., eds., *New Deal Mosaic: Roosevelt Confers with his National Emergency Council.* (Eugene, Oregon: University of Oregon Books, 1965.) The present extract covers pages 374-80 of that source.

Budget. But coming down to legislation, there has never been any clearing house. That is about the size of it, and I think, in the last analysis, that has got to be tied in and go through the Emergency Council. In other words, before you go up there, if you are going to ask for any legislative action, it has got to come through Donald Richberg and up to me if necessary. In all probability, it will come to me. A very good example of that is the Navy. They had a personnel bill, which very properly the Secretary of the Navy sent to me before he went up and asked for this personnel bill on the Hill. Luckily, he did, because the personnel bill as submitted to him by the Department called for two or three hundred Admirals of Fleet and four or five hundred full Admirals, and Rear Admirals, so that everybody would have been an Admiral. We made very short shrift of that, because that comes up every year from the officer of personnel in the Navy. We always step on it. That is just an illustration of the necessity of clearing through the Emergency Council first.

Assistant Secretary Roosevelt [Henry Latrobe Roosevelt, Navy Department]:

We didn't get the Admirals! (*Laughter*)

Secretary Perkins [Department of Labor]:

The difficult problem is that bills are introduced into Congress by any congressman, and he then requests the appearance of the head of the Department to give his views on a particular bill. When the thirty-hour bill is introduced by Mr. Connery, he will certainly desire to know the opinion of the Department of Labor, and I shall postpone appearance just as long as I can. I shall be very busy.

President Roosevelt:

And before you appear, come and talk to Papa.

Secretary Perkins:

But there comes a terrible moment. Do you see?

President Roosevelt:

Yes.

Secretary Perkins:

One is likely to be called on any time. It is very difficult.

President Roosevelt:

You have to use discretion. When you are asked a snap question, you answer with snap judgment at your own peril. The answer may be wrong. I may have to come out and reverse the position. So it is a great deal safer to find out first. It is a great deal easier to say, "I cannot answer that at the present time."

Secretary Morgenthau [Treasury Department]:

One Department should not lobby against another, as it happened last year.

President Roosevelt:

Were there any such cases?

Voice:

Yes, sir!

Another Voice:

Yes, sir!

Another Voice:

YES, SIR! (*Laughter*)

A Member:

It seems to be unanimous.

President Roosevelt:

I wonder if we can lay down a rule. Put that on the agenda for next time.

Mr. Richberg:

There is one matter which is very complicated which I would like to bring out here. We have had a very elaborate study which means weeks of work through a committee representing different departments and agencies in an endeavor to get some coordination in legal activities of the government. There is widespread overlapping and duplication to an extreme extent in the legal divisions and staffs. It has reached the stage where it seems to me it is vitally necessary to get definite organization of a committee headed by a representative of the Attorney General for the purpose of bringing about an elimination of these duplications and use of material. As a matter of fact, one Department studies all over again the same thing another department has got out on that same line. There is no basis of exchange of information, no coordination of the work; and unless that problem is ironed out, we have a great deal of un-necessary duplication. We have a great many suggestions in this pre-liminary report, which was the work largely of a sort of voluntary com-mittee. I think it ought to be organized directly under the Council. My suggestion is that such a committee be appointed, consisting of a representative of the legal staff of each department and agency and headed by a representative of the Attorney General's office to try to bring about a utilization of this study that has already been made.

President Roosevelt:

Do you need any more committees studying it?

Mr. Richberg:

It needs this: a basis for developing policy. I think that group could get together. It involves the question of publication, also. Different departments pay different prices. They do not exchange information. They arrive at opposite opinions.

Judge Biggs [Solicitor General]:

Our department has been working on that subject for some time.

President Roosevelt:

That makes committee number 344!

Mr. Richberg:

This is another committee to eliminate committees!

Mr. Davis [Agricultural Adjustment Administrator]:

Wasn't there a committee appointed on that?

Mr. Richberg:

A committee has been working on it, but it has not been officially settled.

President Roosevelt:

If there is no objection, go ahead and get that going and try to get a report on it early in January, so that I can make a report. I would like to make a report to the Congress on that simplification. You know the tendency to have an independent legal staff in every department. The history is that about every twenty years, our federal and state governments get busy and eliminate a large number of these independent legal staffs with the rather definite objective of concentrating them in the Department of Justice, or whatever it happens to be. About every twenty years you clean house and get rid of a lot of supernumerary lawyers and problems of legal work. I think the twentieth year has come.

Mr. Richberg:

One suggestion that does not require a committee, if it is approved of, is with reference to the Central Statistical Board which exists sort of off by itself. My suggestion is that that should be related directly to the

National Emergency Council by having the Economic Adviser of the Council act as chairman of that Board.

President Roosevelt:

I thought he was.

Mr. Richberg:

It is a peculiar relationship. Mr. Riefler, as a matter of fact, is supplied by the Federal Reserve Board, and if he is going to continue as Economic Adviser, he should be paid through the Council.

President Roosevelt:

Is he paid by the Federal Reserve Board?

Mr. Richberg:

Mr. Eccles presented a memorandum asking why they should pay for a man whose services they do not have.

Member:

He is worth paying!

President Roosevelt:

Is it a question of Civil Service status or anything like that?

Mr. Reifler [Economic Adviser, NEC]:

I have none.

President Roosevelt:

That is unfortunate.

Mr. Richberg:

The Central Statistical Board, of course, is not set up under Executive Order, and if it is made permanent I think the salary ought to come on that budget. That would be the simplest way.

President Roosevelt:

In other words, you come along with the plan of making it a permanent part of the Emergency Council?

Mr. Richberg:

My point is that instead of creating another independent agency, this should be tied in and then it can be called the Statistical Board of the National Emergency Council.

Mr. Bell [Acting Director of the Budget]:

We can budget it that way.

President Roosevelt:

That will relieve the Federal Reserve Board.

Mr. Eccles [Chairman, Federal Reserve Board]:

We wanted Mr. Riefler back; but inasmuch as they are not going to let us have him back, we expect somebody else to pay for him.

President Roosevelt:

We cannot let you have him back. We like him too much.

Secretary Perkins:

Everybody on the board is a working member of the staff of another department and it is highly desirable that that sort of relation should exist. It is one of the few successful pieces of coordination. At the outset it was regarded as very desirable, not only because of his personal qualifications but because of his direct connection with the Federal Reserve, that he head this Board.

Mr. Richberg:

There is no thought of changing that relationship of the board, but this work requires staffing, and that has to be budgeted somewhere. With the Central Statistical Board under the Economic Adviser of the Council and under the Council budget, we could have direct exercise and responsibility, which we have not at the present time. It is off by itself at present. That is my suggestion.

President Roosevelt:

The chorus of approval which met the broad suggestion of the Secretary of the Treasury that no department or agency should go up to the Hill and advocate the things which step on the toes of other departments shows there is a need of saying something about that general situation. Of course that is perfectly true and goes back to something that has been growing for the past six months or a year. And that is the failure of members of the government to mind their own business, to put it roughly; but it is true. You are, all of you, when you receive the press, at a distinct disadvantage; and only a very small percentage of the heads of departments and the heads of agencies know how to handle the press. It is a special art all by itself. They have been doing it all their lives. They have got you at a disadvantage when they start a press conference. Unless you have years of experience in handling it, you will fall into the traps they set for you. There are certain rules in handling the press which I will just give you out of a very wide experience.

If some reporter says to you, "Mr. so-and-so makes such and such a remark (referring to somebody in another department); what do you think of it?" the practice has been to comment upon it in the past, in altogether too many instances. There is a definite reason why you should not, and a definite rule not to comment on it at all. In the first place, it catches you cold; you haven't studied it. In the second place, the quotation that is made to you by this member of the press is so phrased, in many cases, as not to represent what the other department actually said. There are many phases of those questions, many trick ways of putting things. Just for example, last Friday one of the members of the press said, "Mr. President, what have you got today about the speech made by the American Ambassador in England, in which he advocated and suggested a much closer working relationship between Great Britain and the United States?" Obviously, he was trying to get me to say, "Why, I am, of course, in favor of close relationship between Great Britain and the United States." If I had said that at that time, it would have been expressed the next morning that the President advocates a working alliance between the United States and Great Britain. In the middle of the Naval Conference, both Great Britain and the United States having some trouble with Japan, it would have become a sensational story—an Anglo-American Alliance against Japan. On the other hand, if I had said, "I have no comment to make on the speech of the American Ambassador," there would have been a headline intimating that the President had dissented with the remarks of the American Ambassador. Either way I answered that question, I would have been in wrong. I said to the young man, "I have not read the speech of the American Ambassador; I cannot answer any quotation from it which you give from memory, and there is therefore no comment upon it." I did not know what he was trying to do. As a matter of fact, I had read the speech, but I could not remember, snap judgment like that, as to whether this young man was quoting the American Ambassador correctly or not.

Remember always that you are at a disadvantage when the press is talking to you, and remember that when they ask you if what you are doing has some relationship to another department, that it is none of your business without coming to headquarters first to find out. They will say to you, "Such and such a commission or such and such an agency has made such and such a recommendation which seems to affect your department." The answer is, you have nothing to say because you do not know what the recommendation has been; you would like to study it first. The general rule is much the simplest, and that is not to comment about what any of your colleagues are doing. Stick to your own last. If you find something your colleague is doing is actually affecting your department, the Emergency Council and the President are obviously the people to come to to straighten the matter out.

There has been always a great deal of loose talk in Washington. I have met it for years. Remember that when you go out to dinner, the lady that you are sitting next to is probably a sieve to one to three members of the press. Remember everything that you say as a head of a department at a dinner or a dance or a night club will, ten to one, get to the press inside of twelve hours. How does Drew Pearson live, at one extreme; how does Arthur Krock live, at the other extreme? By the gossip that he picks up in Washington. Some of it is gossip that originates from this group right here. And it was spread either by amiable people who are friends of the Drew Pearsons and Arthur Krocks, or it is paid for by them. There are a large number of people, many of them your close friends, many of them my close friends, who actually get paid for giving information to the public press. I am sorry to have to say that. But I know the names of a dozen people who are getting paid for nice, juicy information. You would be surprised if I told you their names.

There is probably no place in the world where the press has closer access to the government than in the city of Washington. We attempt in no way to interfere with the freedom of the press, and at the same time everybody knows that talk outside of the official family is going to be published; and everything you tell a member of Congress is going to be published. There has never been such a thing in the last 50 years as an executive session of the Senate of the United States which is supposed to take up absolutely confidential matters of great public purport so important and so secret that they clear the galleries and put everybody out —I say there has never been an executive session that was not fully public property of the press within half an hour. It is an unfortunate commentary on the Legislative branch. I do not want the Executive branch to have that reputation, but today it has that same reputation. I think the time has come to turn the corner. If anything comes up that affects any other department outside of your own, do not answer it. If your toes are being stepped on, come and tell me. I think that covers it.

Now, before we adjourn, two weeks from today is Christmas Day.

We won't meet that day. When do you want another meeting? How about the end of next week—how would it do to have a meeting on Friday the twenty-first, and then we can adjourn over to the day after New Year's, Wednesday?

Secretary Morgenthau:

Let's not meet on Friday when so many will be wanting to get away for Christmas.

Secretary Perkins:

The four o'clock train is good enough.

Secretary Morgenthau:

But not on the Friday before Christmas.

President Roosevelt:

At the request of the Secretary of the Treasury, we will make it Thursday the twentieth.

Meeting adjourned at 4:10 P.M.

part five

ROOSEVELT
CALLS
FOR
REORGANIZATION

It has been argued above that, although Roosevelt has been most vigorously criticized for his inability or inattention to the institutional problems of administrative management, in fact his record is really quite creditable in this connection. An illustration of the attention FDR *did* give to such problems is printed below. The President's Message to Congress is printed essentially for two reasons. First, in it he summarized the major recommendations of the Brownlow Committee on Administrative Management—some of which would bear fruit in the years to come in the form of an Executive Office of the President and formal budgetary-legislative clearance. Second, it is interesting to note how the President dealt head-on with the classic charge that such recommendations were tantamount to executive usurpation. Roosevelt's essentially conservative, pragmatic, constitutional arguments for reorganization have a charm of their own.

A Call for Reorganization

Franklin D. Roosevelt

To the Congress of the United States:

I address this message to the Congress as one who has had experience as a legislator, as a subordinate in an executive department, as the chief executive of a State, and as one on whom, as President, the constitutional responsibility for the whole of the executive branch of the Government has lain for 4 years.

Now that we are out of the trough of the depression, the time has come to set our house in order. The administrative management of the Government needs overhauling. We are confronted not alone by new activities, some of them temporary in character, but also by the growth of the work of the Government matching the growth of the Nation over more than a generation.

Except for the enactment of the Budget and Accounting Act of 1921, no extensive change in management has occurred since 1913, when the Department of Labor was established. The executive structure of the Government is sadly out of date. I am not the first President to report to the Congress that antiquated machinery stands in the way of effective administration and of adequate control by the Congress. Theodore Roosevelt, William H. Taft, Woodrow Wilson, and Herbert Hoover made repeated but not wholly successful efforts to deal with the problem. Committees of the Congress have also rendered distinguished serv-

President's Committee on Administrative Management, *Report with Special Studies* (Washington, D.C.: Government Printing Office, 1937), pp. iii-v ("Message from the President of the United States").

ice to the Nation through their efforts from time to time to point the way to improvement of governmental management and organization.

The opportunity and the need for action now comes to you and to me. If we have faith in our republican form of government and in the ideals upon which it has rested for 150 years, we must devote ourselves energetically and courageously to the task of making that Government efficient. The great stake in efficient democracy is the stake of the common man.

In these troubled years of world history a self-government cannot long survive unless that government is an effective and efficient agency to serve mankind and carry out the will of the Nation. A government without good management is a house builded on sand.

In striving together to make our Government more efficient, you and I are taking up in our generation the battle to preserve that freedom of self-government which our forefathers fought to establish and hand down to us. They struggled against tyranny, against nonrepresentative controls, against government by birth, wealth, or class, against sectionalism. Our struggle now is against confusion, against ineffectiveness, against waste, against inefficiency. This battle, too, must be won, unless it is to be said that in our generation national self-government broke down and was frittered away in bad management.

Will it be said "Democracy was a great dream, but it could not do the job"? Or shall we here and now, without further delay, make it our business to see that our American democracy is made efficient so that it will do the job that is required of it by the events of our time?

I know your answer, and the answer of the Nation, because, after all, we are a practical people. We know good government in the home, on the farm, and in business, big and little. If any nation can find the way to effective government, it should be the American people through their own democratic institutions.

Over a year ago it seemed to me that this problem of administrative management of the executive branch of the Government should be a major order of business of this session of the Congress. Accordingly, after extended discussions and negotiations, I appointed a Committee on Administrative Management, to examine the whole problem broadly and to suggest for my guidance and your consideration a comprehensive and balanced program for dealing with the overhead organization and management of the executive branch as it is established under the Constitution.

The Committee has now completed its work, and I transmit to you its report, Administrative Management in the Government of the United States. I have examined this report carefully and thoughtfully, and am convinced that it is a great document of permanent importance. I think that the general program presented by the Committee is adequate, reasonable, and practical, and that it furnishes the basis for immediate action. The broad facts are known; the need is clear; what is now required is action.

The Committee on Administrative Management points out that no enterprise can operate effectively if set up as is the Government today. There are over 100 separate departments, boards, commissions, corporations, authorities, agencies, and activities through which the work of the Government is being carried on. Neither the President nor the Congress can exercise effective supervision and direction over such a chaos of establishments, nor can overlapping, duplication, and contradictory policies be avoided.

The Committee has not spared me; they say, what has been common knowledge for 20 years, that the President cannot adequately handle his responsibilities; that he is overworked; that it is humanly impossible, under the system which we have, for him fully to carry out his constitutional duty as Chief Executive, because he is overwhelmed with minor details and needless contacts arising directly from the bad organization and equipment of the Government. I can testify to this. With my predecessors who have said the same thing over and over again, I plead guilty.

The plain fact is that the present organization and equipment of the executive branch of the Government defeats the constitutional intent that there be a single responsible Chief Executive to coordinate and manage the departments and activities in accordance with the laws enacted by the Congress. Under these conditions the Government cannot be thoroughly effective in working, under popular control, for the common good.

The committee does not spare the Comptroller General for his failure to give the Congress a prompt and complete audit each year, totally independent of administration, as a means of holding the Executive truly to account; nor for his unconstitutional assumption of executive power; nor for the failure to keep the accounting system of the Government up to date to serve as the basis of information, management, and control.

The Committee criticizes the use of boards and commissions in administration, condemns the careless use of "corporations" as governmental instrumentalities, and points out that the practice of creating independent regulatory commissions, who perform administrative work in addition to judicial work, threatens to develop a "fourth branch" of the Government for which there is no sanction in the Constitution. Nor does the Committee spare the inadequacy of the civil-service system.

To meet this situation and bring our administrative management up to date, the Committee presents an integrated five-point program, which you will find set out in its report. It includes these major recommendations:

1. Expand the White House staff so that the President may have a sufficient group of able assistants in his own office to keep him in closer and easier touch with the widespread affairs of administration, and to make the speedier clearance of the knowledge needed for Executive decision.

2. Strengthen and develop the managerial agencies of the Government, particularly those dealing with the budget and efficiency research, and personnel and with planning, as management-arms of the Chief Executive.

3. Extend the merit system upward, outward, and downward to cover practically all non-policy-determining posts; reorganize the civil-service system as a part of management under a single, responsible administrator, and create a citizen board to serve as the watch dog of the merit system; and increase the salaries of key posts throughout the service so that the Government may attract and hold in a career service men and women of ability and character.

4. Overhaul the 100 independent agencies, administrations, authorities, boards, and commissions, and place them by Executive order within one or the other of the following 12 major executive departments: State, Treasury, War, Justice, Post Office, Navy, Conservation, Agriculture, Com-

merce, Labor, Social Welfare, and Public Works; and place upon the Executive continuing responsibility for the maintenance of effective organization.

5. Establish accountability of the Executive to the Congress by providing a genuine independent postaudit of all fiscal transactions by an auditor general, and restore to the Executive complete responsibility for accounts and current transactions.

As you will see, this program rests solidly upon the Constitution and upon the American way of doing things. There is nothing in it which is revolutionary, as every element is drawn from our own experience either in government or large-scale business.

I endorse this program and feel confident that it will commend itself to you also with your knowledge of government, and to the vast majority of the citizens of the country who want and believe in efficient self-government.

No important advance can be made toward the major objectives of the program without the passage by the Congress of the necessary legislation.

It will be necessary to provide for the establishment of two new departments, a Department of Social Welfare and a Department of Public Works, for the assignment by the President of all the miscellaneous activities to the 12 major departments thus provided, for reorganization of the civil-service system, for modernizing and strengthening the managerial agencies of the Executive, and for making the Executive more strictly accountable to the Congress. By the creation of two new departments nearly 100 agencies now not under regular departments can be consolidated as to their administrative functions under a total of 12 regular departments of the Government.

The remaining elements of the five-point program, though they must await your action on the basic legislation, may be initiated through appropriations and Executive orders.

In placing this program before you I realize that it will be said that I am recommending the increase of the powers of the Presidency. This is not true. The Presidency as established in the Constitution of the United States has all of the powers that are required. In spite of timid souls in 1787 who feared effective government the Presidency was established as a single strong Chief Executive Office in which was vested the entire executive power of the National Government, even as the legislative power was placed in the Congress, and the judicial in the Supreme Court. What I am placing before you is not the request for more power, but for the tools of management and authority to distribute the work so that the President can effectively discharge those powers which the Constitution now places upon him. Unless we are prepared to abandon this important part of the Constitution, we must equip the Presidency with authority commensurate with his responsibilities under the Constitution.

The Committee on Administrative Management, after a careful examination of recent attempts to reorganize the Government and of State reorganizations carried out so ably by Gov. Frank O. Lowden in Illinois, Gov. Alfred E. Smith in New York, Gov. Harry F. Byrd in Virginia, Gov. William Tudor Gardiner in Maine, and by other governors, accepts the view held by distinguished predecessors that the detailed work of reorganization is, as President Theodore Roosevelt said over 30 years ago, "essentially executive in its nature." The Committee accordingly recommends that reorganization should be a continuing duty and authority of the Chief Executive on the basis of standards set by Congress. To make this safe, the Committee insists, however, that the Congress keep a watchful eye upon reorganization both through the annual budget and through the maintenance of strict executive accountability to the Congress under the independent audit of all financial transactions by an Auditor General. Under the proposed plan the Congress must by law establish the major departments and determine in advance the general principles which shall guide the President in distributing the work of the Government among these departments, and in this task the President is to act on the basis of careful research by the Bureau of the Budget and after conference with those primarily affected. Reorganization is not a mechanical task, but a human task, because government is not a machine, but a living organism. With these clear safeguards, and in view of our past muddling with reorganization, one cannot but accept the logic and wisdom of the recommendations.

I would not have you adopt this five-point program, however, without realizing that this represents an important step in American history.

If we do this, we reduce from over 100 down to a dozen the operating executive agencies of the Government, and we bring many little bureaucracies under broad coordinated democratic authority.

But in so doing, we shall know that we are going back to the Constitution, and giving to the executive branch modern tools of management and up-to-date organization which will enable the Government to go forward efficiently. We can prove to the world that American Government is both democratic and effective.

In this program I invite your cooperation, and pledge myself to deal energetically and promptly with the executive responsibilities of reorganization and administrative management, when you shall have made this possible by the necessary legislation.

FRANKLIN D. ROOSEVELT

THE WHITE HOUSE
January 12, 1937

Suggested Readings

The sources of "Rooseveltiana" are massive. What follows is an exceedingly selective list of works which were particularly useful to the preparation of the essay that introduces this volume. There are three types of sources: the comprehensive histories of FDR and his times; the personal recollections of many of those close to Roosevelt over various lengths of time; and, finally, books about particular problems, aspects, and people connected with the New Deal.

HISTORIES

Burns, James M., *Roosevelt: The Lion and the Fox*. New York: Harcourt, Brace & World, Inc., 1956.

Einaudi, Mario, *The Roosevelt Revolution*. New York: Harcourt, Brace & World, Inc., 1959.

Leuchtenburg, William E., *Franklin D. Roosevelt and the New Deal*. New York: Harper and Row, Publishers, 1963.

Schlesinger, Arthur M., Jr., *The Coming of the New Deal*. Boston: Houghton Mifflin Company, 1959.

————, *The Crisis of the Old Order*. Boston: Houghton Mifflin Company, 1957.

————, *The Politics of Upheaval*. Boston: Houghton Mifflin Company, 1960.

PERSONAL HISTORIES

Blum, John M., *From the Morgenthau Diaries*. Boston: Houghton Mifflin Company, 1959.

Eccles, Marriner, *Beckoning Frontiers*. New York: Alfred A. Knopf, Inc., 1951.

Hull, Cordell, *The Memoirs of Cordell Hull*, 2 vols. New York: The Macmillan Company, 1948.

Ickes, Harold L., *The Secret Diary of Harold L. Ickes*, 3 vols. New York: Simon and Schuster, Inc., 1953, 1954.

Jones, Jesse H., with Edward Angly, *Fifty Billion Dollars*. New York: The Macmillan Company, 1951.

Moley, Raymond, *After Seven Years*. New York: Harper and Row, Publishers, 1939.

Perkins, Frances, *The Roosevelt I Knew*. New York: Harper and Row, Publishers, 1946.

Rosenman, Samuel I., *Working with Roosevelt*. New York: Harper and Row, Publishers, 1952.

Tully, Grace, *F.D.R. My Boss*. New York: Charles Scribner's Sons, 1949.

THE NEW DEAL

Fenno, Richard F., Jr., *The President's Cabinet*. Cambridge, Mass.: Harvard University Press, 1959.

Lindley, Ernest K., *The Roosevelt Revolution: First Phase*. New York: The Viking Press, Inc., 1933.

Lyon, Leverett S., et al., *The National Recovery Administration*. Washington, D.C.: The Brookings Institution, 1935.

Macmahon, Arthur W., John D. Millet, and Gladys Ogden, *The Administration of Federal Work Relief*. Chicago: Public Administration Service, 1941.

Neustadt, Richard E., *Presidential Power: The Politics of Leadership*. New York: John Wiley & Sons, Inc., 1960.

Sherwood, Robert, *Roosevelt and Hopkins*. New York: Harper and Row, Publishers, 1948.

Timmons, Bascom N., *Jesse Jones, The Man and the Statesman.* New York: Holt, Rinehart & Winston, Inc., 1956.

Tugwell, Rexford G., *The Democratic Roosevelt.* Garden City, N.Y.: Doubleday and Company, 1957.